Beading
LEARN IT • LOVE IT

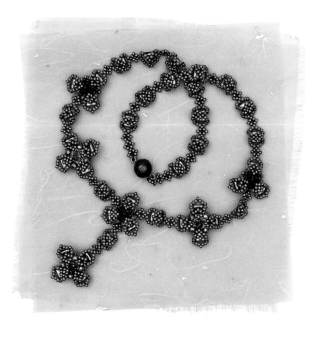

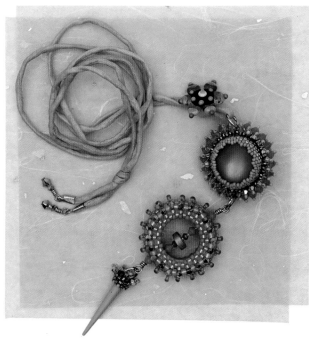

Beading
LEARN IT · LOVE IT

JEAN POWER

BARRON'S

Contents

Beading. Learn It. Love It.
A QUARTO BOOK

Copyright © 2015 Quarto Inc.

First edition for North America published in 2016 by Barron's Educational Series, Inc.

All inquiries should be addressed to:
Barron's Educational Series, Inc.
250 Wireless Boulevard
Hauppauge, New York 11788
www.barronseduc.com

ISBN: 978-1-4380-0758-8

Library of Congress Control No.:
2015948411

QUAR.BCTH

Conceived, designed, and produced by
Quarto Publishing plc
The Old Brewery
6 Blundell Street
London N7 9BH

Senior editor: Katie Crous
Art editor & designer: Julie Francis
Art director: Caroline Guest
Picture research: Sarah Bell,
   Georgia Cherry
Photographer: Simon Pask
Copy editor: Diana Craig
Proofreader: Sarah Hoggett

Creative director: Moira Clinch
Publisher: Paul Carslake

Color separation by PICA Digital Pte
   Ltd, Singapore
Printed in China by 1010 Printing
   International Limited

9 8 7 6 5 4 3 2 1

Welcome ...

Ever since I made my first pair of earrings when I was a teenager, I have been captivated by beads and the delightful things that can be made with them. Their colors, sparkle, and versatility all combine to make me want to learn as many ways to use them as possible, and it is this curiosity and subsequent knowledge that form the basis of this book.

Although I am known for specializing in bead weaving, often with small beads, my love of jewelry making also covers wirework and stringing. I enjoy mixing media to achieve different results, and within different timeframes—using all three methods makes both of these things possible.

Within the pages of this book I have included all of the basic instructions, along with tips, tricks, and expert knowledge that will help you to design and create the style of jewelry you want to make. By following my guidance, and with a little bit of practice, you'll be able to achieve a high level of finish and begin creating jewelry you'll be proud to wear or gift to others.

JEAN POWER

About this book

The core of this book takes each principal category of beaded jewelry-making—Stringing, Wirework, and Beadwork—and covers in depth the related materials, knowledge, skills, and techniques.

CHAPTER 1
Beads, findings, and tools
PAGES 8–19

All the essential beads, findings, tools, and rules of design can be found here, so make it your first port of call, especially if you are new to beading.

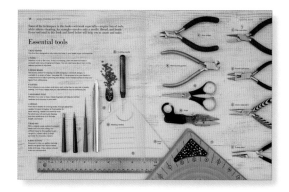

BE INSPIRED

Each section features a gallery of work from professional bead jewelry makers, offering inspiration and background information on how the piece was made.

CHAPTERS 2, 3, AND 4
Stringing, wirework, and beadwork
PAGES 20–153

The three foundational elements of making beaded jewelry are covered here, and the pages contain a wealth of learning devices to help you tackle new areas of your craft with knowledge and confidence.

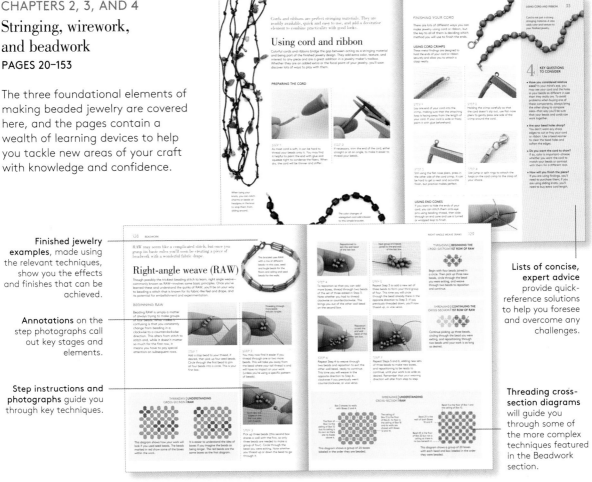

Finished jewelry examples, made using the relevant techniques, show you the effects and finishes that can be achieved.

Annotations on the step photographs call out key stages and elements.

Step instructions and photographs guide you through key techniques.

Lists of concise, expert advice provide quick-reference solutions to help you foresee and overcome any challenges.

Threading cross-section diagrams will guide you through some of the more complex techniques featured in the Beadwork section.

QUICK START AND GUEST DESIGNER PROJECTS

Test your new-found skills with the projects at the end of each section. The Quick start projects are designed to get you off the mark quickly and efficiently. The Guest designer projects (see right) show you how talented, professional bead jewelers work, and provide you with an opportunity to take your skills to a higher level.

Step illustrations show you the main stages of the project and provide threading paths where necessary or relevant.

The relevant techniques that feature in the book are highlighted at the start of each Guest Designer project, so that you can refer to the relevant technique in the book.

Beads, findings, and tools

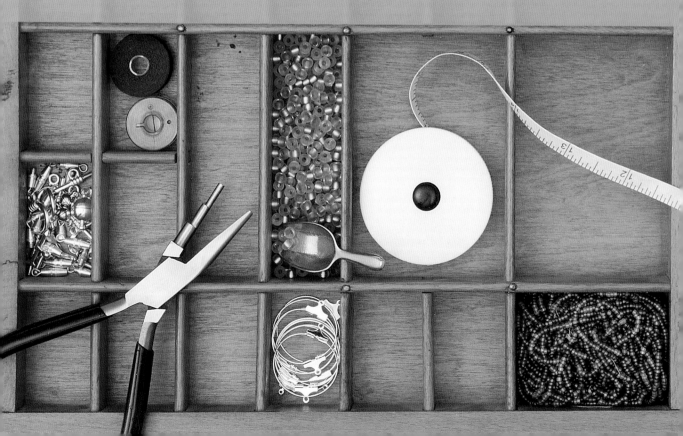

This chapter provides a visual introduction to some of the most useful bead types and the essential tools and findings you'll need to make string, wirework, or beaded jewelry. Learn about color theory and the fundamental elements of good jewelry design to ensure that your beaded creations are both practical and beautiful.

Beads are an ancient artform, and even the modern methods of using them have developed from ancient ways. All the beads available to purchase today have grown from the most basic of beads that was first used: a simple pebble or shell with a hole in it. Developments in manufacturing, trade, science, and fashion have all influenced the beads we now have at our fingertips.

Beginning with the beads

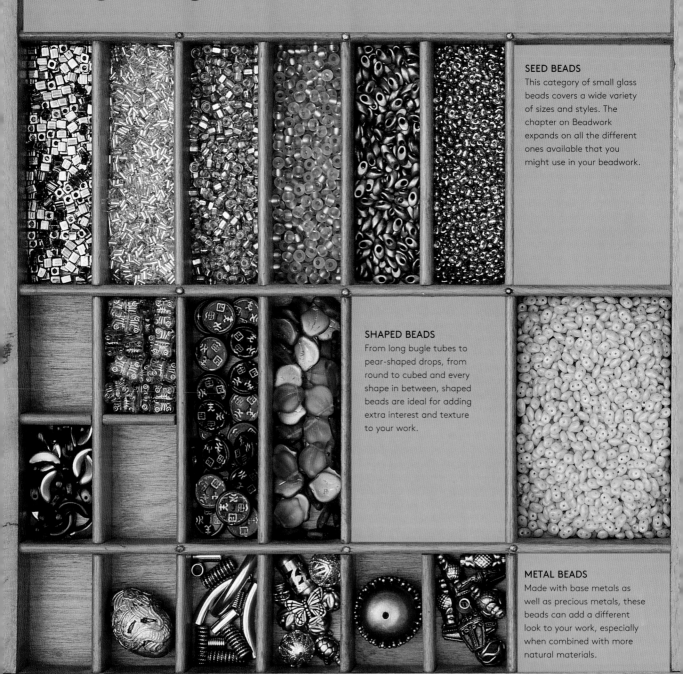

SEED BEADS
This category of small glass beads covers a wide variety of sizes and styles. The chapter on Beadwork expands on all the different ones available that you might use in your beadwork.

SHAPED BEADS
From long bugle tubes to pear-shaped drops, from round to cubed and every shape in between, shaped beads are ideal for adding extra interest and texture to your work.

METAL BEADS
Made with base metals as well as precious metals, these beads can add a different look to your work, especially when combined with more natural materials.

CRYSTALS

Crystals, manmade or otherwise, are ideal for adding sparkle and shine to your jewelry making. Available in different shapes, sizes, and colors, they are often cut with many facets to reflect light and exaggerate their shine.

PEARLS AND SHELLS

Whether grown naturally in the wild or cultured, pearls are a classic component for strung jewelry, and wirework and beading can be added for a modern twist. You may find that your pearls and shell beads have very small holes, and the shells in particular can have sharp holes. A bead reamer is ideal for dealing with both of these issues.

WOODEN BEADS

Available in various shapes and sizes, wooden beads can be bought already dyed or plain, so you can decorate them yourself.

SEMI-PRECIOUS BEADS

These affordable gemstones are available in as many variations as Mother Nature made, and sometimes with a little extra help from man to perk up their color. Be aware that gemstone beads often have very small stringing holes. This is to reduce the chance of breakage when they're made, and if you need or want to increase the hole size, then a bead reamer will help.

LAMPWORK BEADS

Lampworking, sometimes called flameworking, is the act of forming hot rods of glass over metal rods in a flame to make glass beads. Though these can be bought cheaply, more expensive ones sold by lampwork artists have been annealed (heated and then cooled to specific temperatures) to make them more crack resistant.

"Findings" is the term for all those little pieces of metal that help to turn your bag of beads into wonderful jewelry creations. Designed for a variety of uses, the basic idea is to use them to finish your work securely, neatly, and easily.

Essential findings

1 CLASPS

Clasps close and secure your jewelry while it's being worn. Once you add in size, shape, and color variations to the basic style, there are hundreds of clasps on the market. Which one you choose depends on your personal tastes, your budget, and the design you're making. Experiment with different clasps to see the different looks they give you, and keep your eye out in charity or thrift stores for broken or otherwise unattractive necklaces with lovely vintage clasps.

2 EARRING FINDINGS

Like clasps, there are many different earrings findings on the market, both for pierced and non-pierced ears. They can vary in style from practical to more ornately designed, should you want them to be the center of attention.

3 JUMP AND SPLIT RINGS

These small loops of metal are ideal for attaching findings to your work. Jump rings are single loops and split rings are multiple loops, similar to what you might find on a keyring.

4 CRIMP BEADS, CORD CRIMPS, CLAMSHELLS, AND COVERS

When stringing with cord or beading wire, you need a way to both finish the work and to attach your strung piece to a clasp. These findings are designed just for that job. You can find out more about them in the Stringing section.

5 FRENCH WIRE

This fine wire coil, which is made from gold or silver wire, was originally designed to protect stringing thread from wearing against metal clasps when used with pearl knotting. However, you can also use it when bead weaving to protect your beading thread from rubbing and breaking.

6 HEAD PINS

These lengths of wire, with a flattened or decorative end, stop your beads from falling off, and are useful for making charms or dangles, by attaching them to your work with simple or wrapped loops.

7 EYE PINS

These lengths of wire are similar to head pins, but have a loop at one end from which you can hang beads.

Some of the techniques in this book—wirework especially—require lots of tools, while others—beading, for example—involve only a needle, thread, and beads. Every tool used in this book and listed below will help you to create and make.

Essential tools

1 BEAD REAMER
This fine file is designed to help make the holes in your beads larger and smoother.

2 PLIERS
Whether round or flat-nose, 3-step or crimping, pliers are essential tools in wirework and many stringing techniques. You can read more about them in the relevant sections in this book.

3 DESIGN BOARD
This board, perfect for helping you with stringing or wirework designs, is available in a variety of sizes (see page 18). It has grooves to lay your beads in, measurements to help in planning your design, and a flocked surface to stop your beads from rolling away.

4 CUTTERS
From scissors to wire cutters and more, each cutter has its own role in jewelry making. You'll soon realize that you need different ones for different jobs.

5 MEASURING TOOLS
Whether it's a ruler or tape, measuring tools will help you achieve neatness and accuracy in your work.

6 NEEDLES
From blunt needles for moving knots, through extra-fine needles for pearl stringing, to fine needles for bead weaving, needles are essential tools for which you will eventually develop your own preference as to the size, length, and brand.

7 BEAD MAT
With a slightly rough surface to prevent beads and wire from rolling, but without loops for the needles to get caught in, a bead mat is a smart purchase for all jewelry makers.

8 BEAD SCOOPS
Designed to help you gather roaming beads and place them back in bead tubes and bags, these various-shaped tools are indispensable.

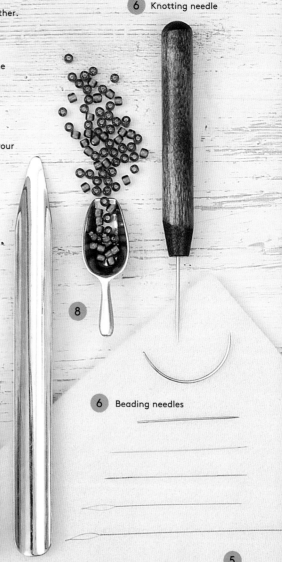

6 Knotting needle

8

6 Beading needles

5

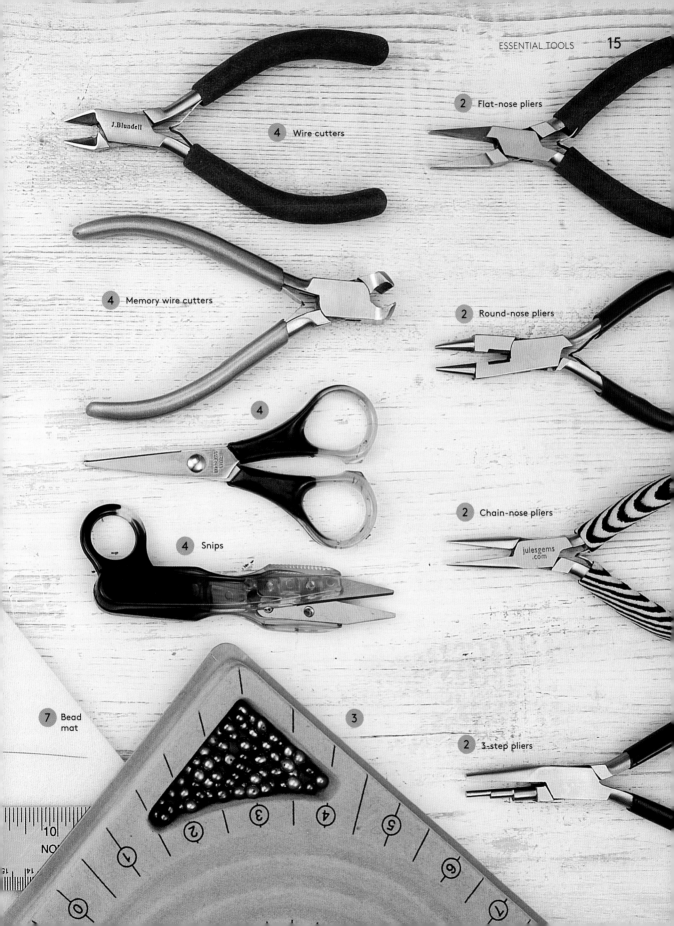

4 Wire cutters

2 Flat-nose pliers

4 Memory wire cutters

2 Round-nose pliers

4

4 Snips

2 Chain-nose pliers

julesgems
.com

7 Bead
   mat

3

2 3-step pliers

A lot of emphasis is placed on technique, but design is just as important. Giving extra thought to the form, color, and shape of your jewelry will enhance the look and feel of the finished piece. Combining great color schemes with texture and interest will result in creating exceptional designs.

Design considerations

WORKING WITH COLOR

What attracts you first when you walk into a bead store? For many, it's the color of the beads; chances are, you are the same. Led by instinct, you will automatically be drawn to the beads of your favorite color, and there is nothing wrong with that! But you need to know how to put your chosen colors together.

THE COLOR WHEEL

A color wheel is an invaluable tool for anyone designing jewelry with beads and wire. Colors are organized on the wheel to show the relationships between them. Use the color wheel to understand how different colors can work together.

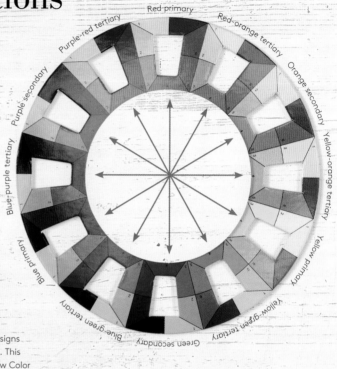

There are several color wheel designs available in any art supply store. This example is based on the Rainbow Color Selector, courtesy of K1C2, LLC.

FOUNDATIONAL COLOR SCHEMES

In jewelry making, experimenting with different schemes can be satisfying when you come up with something new that you love. The following "foundation schemes" are great places to start.

1 ANALOGOUS COLORS

Analogous schemes use three harmonious colors that are found next to each other on the wheel—for example, green, turquoise, and blue. Harmony is achieved because all the colors are similar. These are easy yet effective schemes to put together, allowing variety in color without the jolting contrasts.

2 MONOCHROMATIC COLORS

In these tints, shades, and tones of a single hue, beads based on one color but with different textures and finishes work well together. Small accents of a pure hue can also be added, using monochromatic colors to add highlights.

3 COMPLEMENTARY COLORS

On opposite sides of the wheel, complementary colors—for example, red and green—produce the greatest contrast when placed together. The contrast brings out the colors of the beads. Often, the best results are achieved by using varying amounts of the colors—for example, by using a main color and a smaller amount of a complementary color as an accent.

4 SPLIT COMPLEMENTARY

This scheme uses one color plus the two colors on either side of its complementary color on the wheel—for instance, red with blue-green and yellow-green, or yellow-orange with blue and purple. Either the main color or its two complementaries should dominate—equal proportions of the three colors could be jarring.

5 TRIADIC COLORS

These are an equilateral triangle of colors from the wheel—for example, all three primaries or all three secondaries. The proportion of the three colors you choose is important; if the colors clash, then it is best to tone them down. One color should dominate, while the third could be used as an accent color.

6 HARMONIOUS COLORS

Colors that are said to be in "harmony" sit within any quarter of the wheel. Draw a circle to the same size as the color wheel, and cut out one quarter. Placing this on top of the wheel, and turning it around, shows the harmonious sections clearly.

7 TEMPERATURE

Warm colors—reds and oranges—are dominant; cool colors—blues and violets—tend to be recessive. If two colors of equal temperature are placed together, they vibrate. The temperature is altered by background colors. If the background is warm, then the color appears cooler; and if cool, it appears warmer. Even when using colors lying opposite each other on the wheel (a complementary scheme), you can still achieve an overall warm feeling as long as you use more of the warm colors and less of the cool ones.

Multi-colored pieces can make use of the whole color spectrum. Tints and shades of the same colors help to vary the tone.

8 TETRADIC COLORS

Tetradic colors are four colors at the corners of a square or rectangle placed on the wheel. The colors are arranged into two complementary pairs. The strong visual contrast also works well if one color dominates and the others complement each other. For a pleasing result, keep similar tones together—so if you use a blue-green, also use a blue-purple rather than a pure green or a pure purple.

9 BLACK AND WHITE

Technically, black and white are not colors but they can still have eye-popping results. Black doesn't reflect as much light as white does; therefore the contrast and relationship between these two tones can produce stunning and dramatic looks.

A selection of color schemes in action is shown opposite. Partly it's down to personal taste but some color combinations are just more pleasing than others.

CREATING LAYOUTS WITH A DESIGN BOARD

Laying out the beads and materials for your design allows you to test the look of the finished piece. Bead design boards are creative yet practical spaces in which you can experiment with the color, shape, size, and length of your beads before you string them all together into a final piece.

There are many different types of beading boards, but most of them have one or more long grooves or channels around the board, marked with numbers or lines, where you lay out your beads. Once you have placed your beads into the compartments, the design fun begins.

The easiest way to start is with a central bead and then work your way to the ends. Rearrange your beads until you are completely happy with your design. If you have a beading board with a few channels, you can make more than one sample and keep them in the channels next to each other to see which one you prefer.

If different-sized beads are used, it's important to keep a balance by placing the largest bead in the middle—in this case, the donut-shaped tiger-eye bead.

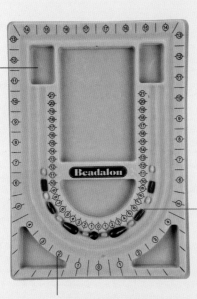

Containers: Useful indentations hold beads and findings as you work.

The grooves: Placing your beads in the grooves will help you to plan the individual strands of your finished piece. Experiment with color choices and the order of your beads here. Most bead design boards come with three grooves, which enables you to plan a multi-strand piece and see how the different strands will interact.

Measurements: Around the outside and inside edges of the board are measurements to help you work out the exact length of your piece. When laying your beads on the board, make sure you don't leave any gaps, as this will give you an inaccurate length.

FUNDAMENTAL ELEMENTS OF DESIGN

Understanding how size, shape, balance, and weight work together is at the heart of successful bead jewelry design. These are the design fundamentals that help to create stunning designs that are comfortable to wear.

SIZE

The size element of design includes the size of the finished piece as well as the dimensions of the individual beads. Not only are these important features in their own right, but the ratio between the two will dramatically alter the appearance of a piece of jewelry.

SHAPE

Factor the shape of the beads, as well as the shape of the finished piece, into your designs. The shape of the individual beads will influence the end design as well as determine the weight and wearability of the finished piece. When you select feature beads, the shape of beads is also important.

Lots of small irregular beads, such as the fluorite and quartz crystals in this necklace, will create a highly textured effect; however, this may be uncomfortable to wear close to the skin.

Balance is particularly important with necklaces that are designed to fall a certain way. The drop crystals of this lariat serve as weights to pull the otherwise light strands so they sit attractively.

BALANCE

Balance includes making sure that the weight, as well as the look of a piece of jewelry, is well balanced. Balance does not mean that an item needs to be structured or formal in design. Creating striking asymmetrical jewelry, for instance, involves considering how balance affects the design. If the weight is balanced incorrectly, the necklace may twist. Finding a solution that offers both visual and physical balance can be a matter of compromise.

WEIGHT

The weight of a piece of jewelry will affect how comfortable it is to wear. This will also influence how a piece hangs or sits in place. Weight is particularly important to factor into designs for earrings, as heavy earrings can pull on the lobes. Individual beads will also impact the finished weight of an item. By altering the size or material of the beads, you may be able to change the weight of the finished item.

7 | PRINCIPAL BEAD FINISHES

The surface finish of a bead will have a significant effect in a design. Matte beads absorb light, while shiny beads reflect light and sparkle. Mixing finishes is a great way to add texture and variation to a design.

Fire-polished faceted rounds, transparent

- **Transparent:** These beads transmit light, and you can see through them clearly. This means that their colors tend to be muted unless placed against a background.

Pressed glass beads

- **Translucent:** These beads also transmit light; you can see through them a little but not clearly. They have a more muted appearance than transparent beads.

Opal faceted crystals

- **Opal:** These beads transmit some light and have a very milky finish. The effect is a subtle and soft appearance.

Opaque faceted crystals

- **Opaque:** These beads don't transmit light; you can't see through them. Their bold color and design would stand out in a finished piece.

Freshwater pearls

- **Satin:** These beads are silky to the touch and tactile. They are versatile and work well with both matte and gloss beads.

Silver acrylic beads

- **Metallic:** These beads have a shiny, galvanized (coated) finish, which may wear off over time. Metallic finishes add a sense of luxury and glitz to a design.

Matte painted beads (unvarnished)

- **Matte:** These beads are non-gloss or frosted and tend to recede into the background rather than jump out.

CHAPTER 2

Stringing

Putting beads on a string might seem basic, but it has many possibilities. Learn how to use different cords, ribbons, and threads to create jewelry that can range from a simple elastic bracelet to a multi-strand choker. Combine beads with decorative knots and discover how to use findings for a professional finish.

1

2

3

4

Stringing:
be inspired

1. CHRIS & JOY POUPAZIS A rugged look can be achieved with large, uneven rock gems. Specially-made charms add decoration, and gold-plated beads complement the dark brown smoky quartz. These gems were picked carefully to match, while also providing contrast with their different shapes and sizes.

2. KIMBERLY HOUSTON Kimberly used a variety of simply strung beads in this bracelet. Lampwork beads, beaded beads, Bali sterling silver beads, and crystal beads combine for high impact.

5

3. LYNDA CARSON Combine nature-inspired colors and natural-looking beads for a boho necklace with style. Lynda used orange-dyed jade rounds with wooden discs, rounds, and crescent beads.

4. LYNN DAVY Combining seed beads, accents, and metal components results in a multi-stranded, textural necklace that displays a gorgeous, handmade lampwork focal bead to full advantage.

5. CHRIS & JOY POUPAZIS The six strands of pearls and gems that make up this elegant necklace are secured with crimps. A lobster claw clasp secures the strands onto the chain, which allows the wearer to turn the piece into a belt, if preferred.

6

7

8

9

6. LYNDA CARSON Chalcedony and lampwork beads combine on handknotted Irish waxed linen cord to make this attractive, rustic-style bracelet. A decorative clasp made of tiny seed beads links to an artisan copper button.

7. CHRIS & JOY POUPAZIS Color, shape, and texture all play a key part in the design of this asymmetrical necklace. Ten-strand jewelry wire makes up the main part of the piece, with a second 7-strand wire of smaller beads weaved at random and punctuated with handmade charms.

8. CHRIS & JOY POUPAZIS Designing for versatility gives the wearer options; here, the tiger-eye, sea bamboo, and crystal necklace can be worn long or as a choker due to its extension chain, which allows the clasp to be fastened at a variety of points.

9. CAROL BLACKBURN This polymer necklace combines blended cone beads with small gold spacer beads. The graduating warm tones are a prime example of successful color work.

10

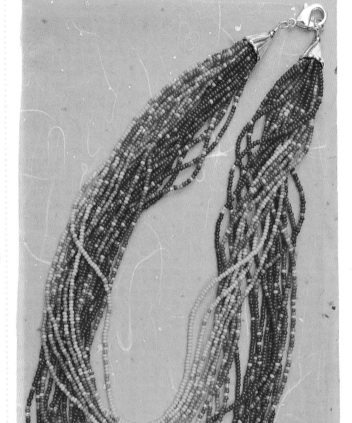

11

12

10. KIMBERLY HOUSTON The rose and its accompanying dangles provide a strong focal point for this coordinated bracelet on beading elastic.

11. LYNN DAVY This striking bracelet makes the most of a few special beads by framing them with bunches of tactile dangles. A single big heart adds the perfect finishing touch.

12. LYNN DAVY The vibrant effect of this fire-inspired necklace is achieved with only four different colors of seed beads, a sprinkling of crystals, and clever use of a bead spinner, proving that you don't have to learn complicated beadweaving stitches in order to make something amazing with tiny beads.

Stringing covers a wide range of techniques and materials, all designed to help you take some thread and beads and turn them into beautiful pieces of jewelry. These essential tools and materials will help make your work easier.

Essential stringing tools and supplies

1 BEAD REAMER
Many gemstones and pearls have very small holes, so this tool (a small file) is perfect for making your bead holes larger and for removing sharp edges.

2 CRIMPING PLIERS
Designed to crimp and round your crimp beads, these pliers can be replaced by flat-nose pliers, but using the correct tool will give you a better result.

3 BEADING ELASTIC
Designed especially for jewelry, beading elastic is available in a variety of widths and comes in either clear or black. It is finished using an overhand or square knot (see pages 28–29).

4 BEADING WIRE
Multiple strands of fine stainless steel, coated in nylon, make this stringing material strong and durable. Combined with crimp beads, beading wire makes a quick and easy method of stringing.

5 JUMP AND SPLIT RINGS
These small loops of metal are ideal to attach your stringing and your findings.

6 MEMORY WIRE
With its strength and ability to hold a shape, memory wire makes for an ideal stringing material when you don't want to use a clasp.

7 CORD AND RIBBON
Available in many different colors, materials, textures, and widths, cord is ideal for adding a new look to your work. Satin rattail, available in 1 or 2mm diameters, is the most common cord used in jewelry making.

8 DESIGN BOARD
Designed to help you plan out your piece, the grooves in this board help you lay out your beads to see how they'll look before you start stringing.

9 CRIMP BEADS AND COVERS
Designed to combine with beading wire, these metal beads are crimped onto the wire to grip the nylon securely. Crimp covers are like a clamshell, closing over the crimp to hide it.

10 FRENCH WIRE
This fine wire coil is made from gold or silver wire and is designed to protect your stringing thread from wearing against your metal clasp.

11 BLUNT NEEDLE OR AWL
These are perfect for helping you slide your overhand knots into the exact position you need.

12 CORD CRIMPS
These findings are designed to be crimped onto the ends of your cord so that you can attach a clasp using the attaching loop.

13 CLAMSHELLS
Shaped like small clamshells, these metal findings are designed to be closed over a knot or crimp at the end of your thread or beading wire.

14 FINE NEEDLES OR FINE WIRE
Pearls and gemstones have very small threading holes, so the techniques used to string them often involve using a doubled thread. A very fine needle, purchased or home-made, will fit through your bead holes and can be cut off when it is no longer needed.

15 STRINGING THREAD
Made of silk, nylon, or similar material, bead stringing thread is fine but strong, and comes in a variety of thicknesses and colors.

QUESTIONS TO HELP YOU CHOOSE THE RIGHT STRINGING OPTION

- **Do you know the finished size of your project?** If not, then memory wire, elastic, or cord with sliding knots is perfect.

- **Are your bead holes small?** Then beading wire and crimps of thread with knots are ideal.

- **Will the wearer struggle to use a clasp?** Then choose memory wire or elastic, as neither require a clasp.

- **Is the jewelry for a child?** If so, you want something that will come off easily. Memory wire or elastic is a suitable choice—do not use something strong such as beading wire and crimps.

- **Are the beads fragile?** Then beading thread with knots between each bead will help to protect them from hitting each other.

- **Do the beads have large holes?** If so, cord is easy to use and means the beads won't flop around on the stringing material.

Whether you use elastic, thread, or cord, knowing how to tie
a knot is essential to your jewelry-making repertoire.

Essential jewelry knots

Knots can be simple or intricate, decorative or practical, small or large, but their
basic elements are the same, no matter which you use or why you use them.
Whether you're looking to secure your beading elastic or to add extra color to
a cord necklace, these three knots are all you need.

LARK'S HEAD KNOT

Simple to tie, the lark's head knot
is great to use when hanging
pendants from cords or ribbons.

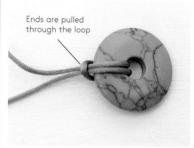

Ends are pulled
through the loop

STEP 1
Fold the cord or ribbon in half to form
a loop. Thread the loop though the
hole in the pendant. Note that
threading from front to back will give
you a different look than threading
from back to front.

STEP 2
Bring the ends of the cord through the
loop and pull to tighten and neaten
the knot.

OVERHAND KNOT

This knot is easy to tie and will
probably come naturally to you.
Think of it as the knot you would
tie at the end of a balloon.

STEP 1
Fold the cord, or cords, over to form
a loop.

STEP 2
Thread the ends of the cord through
the loop and pull to tighten.

This necklace uses knots in the cord both as a decorative device and to lengthen the necklace.

SQUARE KNOT

Also known as a reef knot, this is a more secure variation of a granny knot (a binding knot, used to secure a rope or line around an object).

STEP 1
Arrange the ends of the cord or ribbon with the left-hand end over the right.

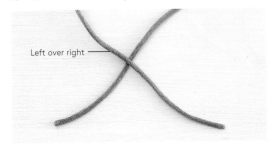

Left over right

STEP 2
Wrap the left-hand end under the right-hand end and then bring back on top.

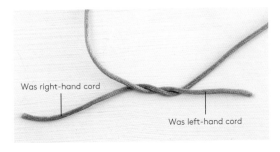

Was right-hand cord

Was left-hand cord

STEP 3
Lay what is now the right-hand end over the left, then wrap it under the left and pull up to the top again. Pull to tighten.

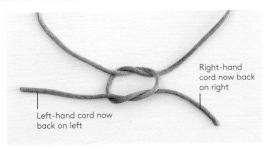

Left-hand cord now back on left

Right-hand cord now back on right

2 WAYS TO PERFECT KNOTS

- **If a knot isn't in the right place, you can move it before it's fully tightened.** Insert a blunt needle into the knot and slide it to where you want the knot.

- **Always do a knot test.** Gently check your knots before you rely on them. It's better to have your work come apart on your beading mat than while it's being worn.

6 GREAT REASONS TO USE KNOTS

- **To finish a piece of jewelry.** For example, when using beading elastic.

- **To add security.** Adding knots between pearls or beads means that if the string breaks, you won't lose all of them at once.

- **To protect your beads.** Adding knots between beads will separate them and prevent them from knocking against each other.

- **To add a decorative feature.** As well as having a practical function, knots can be a design element in their own right, so experiment to see what you can create—and if you choose colorful cord, you'll be adding another decorative feature.

- **To provide additional length.** Adding knots to your stringing material will create a longer piece of jewelry than if the beads were simply strung.

- **To hold beads in place.** Tying a knot in your stringing material either side of a bead or charm will stop it from sliding around.

Quick, easy to use, and versatile, beading elastic is an ideal material to add to your jewelry-making kit. Use it wisely and soon you'll have pieces that are pleasing to look at and fun to wear.

Using elastic

Once you have learned the secret of how to tie knots in beading elastic, you'll be able to string jewelry in no time at all. Its low cost and ease of use also mean that you can use it to string several beads quickly and enjoy wearing them even while deciding the final finished look.

USING AN OVERHAND KNOT

Slide the knot to the beads.

STEP 1
Hold the ends of the elastic together. Make sure you have pushed the beads along the elastic so that there are no gaps between them.

STEP 2
Make a loop with the ends of the elastic. Pull the ends through the loop and tie the knot.

STEP 3
If necessary, use a large, blunt needle to slide the knot up against the beads. Tighten the knot by pulling on the ends of the elastic. Make sure that the knot is secure, then trim.

USING A SQUARE KNOT

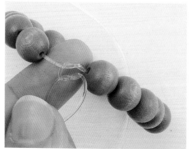

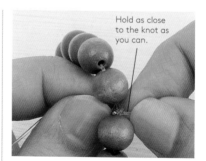
Hold as close to the knot as you can.

STEP 1
Bring the two ends of the elastic together. Lay the left-hand end over the right, then pull it through the central gap.

STEP 2
Lay what is now the left-hand side over the right-hand side and pull the ends through the gap created.

STEP 3
Pull on both ends of the elastic to tighten and secure the knot. To fully tighten it, make sure you pull as close to the knot as possible.

These colorful bracelets were strung in minutes and can be mixed and matched as you see fit.

HIDING THE KNOT

STEP 1
Simply slide a large-holed bead over the knot tied in the elastic to hide it from view.

STEP 2
If the bead slides off the knot, you can add a touch of glue to the bead hole and secure the knot in the bead so that it remains hidden.

4 GOOD PRACTICES TO FOLLOW

- **Choose the right size.** Beading elastic comes in 0.5, 0.7, and 1mm widths. The thickest width is the easiest to use, holds its stretch better, and is easier to knot. But if you're threading on beads with small holes, you may need to choose a finer option.

- **Protect the elastic.** Any sharp edges along the holes in the beads can cut through the elastic. A bead reamer is perfect for softening these edges.

- **Get in close.** When tightening a knot, you need to hold the elastic as close to the knot as possible. Holding it farther away and then trying to tighten will mean you're stretching the elastic more than tightening the knot.

- **Test for tightness.** Once you've tied your knot, gently test the elastic to see if it holds. Don't pull on the elastic too hard, as your beads may go everywhere. Instead, look closely and, if there's any movement, tighten the knot again until it is secure.

This Wild Mustang bracelet by Kimberley Houston uses simple stringing on beading elastic, and teams Czech glass with Arizona Chrysocolla, silver plate, and a pewter horse charm.

Cords and ribbons are perfect stringing materials. They are readily available, quick and easy to use, and add a decorative element to combine practicality with good looks.

Using cord and ribbon

Colorful cords and ribbons bridge the gap between acting as a stringing material and being part of the finished jewelry design. They add extra color, texture, and interest to any piece and are a great addition in a jewelry maker's toolbox. Whether they are an added extra or the focal point of your jewelry, you'll soon discover lots of ways to play with them.

PREPARING THE CORD

STEP 1
As most cord is soft, it can be hard to thread your beads onto it. You may find it helpful to paint the end with glue and squeeze tight to condense the fibers. When dry, the cord will be thinner and stiffer.

STEP 2
If necessary, trim the end of the cord, either straight or at an angle, to make it easier to thread your beads.

When tying your knots, you can catch charms or beads on head pins in the knot to stop them from sliding around.

The color changes of variegated cord add interest to this simple bracelet.

FINISHING YOUR CORD

There are lots of different ways you can make jewelry using cord or ribbon, but the key to all of them is deciding which method you will use to finish the ends.

USING CORD CRIMPS
These metal findings are designed to hold the ends of your cord or ribbon securely and allow you to attach a clasp neatly.

STEP 1
Lay one end of your cord into the crimp, making sure that the attaching loop is facing away from the length of your cord. If your cord is wide or frizzy, paint it with glue beforehand.

STEP 2
Holding the crimp carefully so that the cord doesn't slip out, use flat-nose pliers to gently press one side of the crimp around the cord.

STEP 3
Still using the flat-nose pliers, press in the other side of the cord crimp. It can be hard to get a neat and accurate finish, but practice makes perfect.

STEP 4
Use jump or split rings to attach the loops on the cord crimp to the clasp of your choice.

USING END CONES
If you want to hide the ends of your cord, you can stitch them onto eye pins using beading thread, then slide through an end cone and use a turned or wrapped loop to finish.

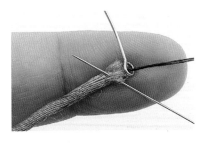

Cord is not just a strong stringing material—it also adds color and texture to your finished jewelry.

4 | KEY QUESTIONS TO CONSIDER

- **Have you considered relative sizes?** In your mind's eye, you may see your cord and the holes in your beads as different in size than they really are. To avoid problems when buying one of these components, always bring the other along to compare sizes—that way you'll be sure that your beads and cords can work together.

- **Are your bead holes sharp?** You don't want any sharp edges to cut or fray your cord or ribbon. Use a bead reamer to clear the bead holes and soften the edges.

- **Do you want the cord to show?** If so, color is important—choose whether you want the cord to match your beads or contrast with them for a different look.

- **How will you finish the piece?** If you are using findings, you'll need to purchase them; if you are using sliding knots, you'll need to buy extra cord length.

SLIDING KNOTS

Sliding knots allow you to make a necklace or bracelet without a clasp that can be adjusted to different sizes. The sliding knots allow you to open the piece of jewelry wide enough to put it on and then tighten it to wear. As you do this, bear in mind that you're not knotting the ends of the cords together—instead, you're tying a knot in each end so that the other end can slide through the knot.

Colorful ribbon can be treated as cord and used as a stringing material, as shown in this necklace.

SIMPLE SLIDING KNOTS

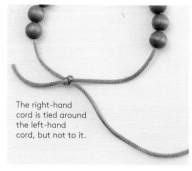

The right-hand cord is tied around the left-hand cord, but not to it.

STEP 1
String your piece, but leave plenty of cord at each end. Lay the whole piece down on a flat surface and slightly overlap the ends.

STEP 2
Using an overhand knot, tie one end of the cord around the other end to form a circle. Pull tight to secure, but not so tight that your knot can't slide along the cord.

STEP 3
Using an overhand knot, tie the other end of the cord to the circle, pulling the knot tight but allowing it to slide along the cord.

ADVANCED SLIDING KNOTS

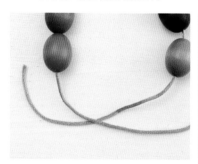

STEP 1
String your piece, but leave plenty of cord at each end. Lay the whole piece down on a flat surface and slightly overlap the ends. You need about 5 in (13cm) of cord on each end for you to tie the knots easily.

STEP 2
Take one of the cord ends and loop it back on itself. You're now going to wrap the cord, starting to wrap 1 in (2cm) from the loop end.

STEP 3
Wrap the cut end of the cord around the folded-over cord and the other length of cord (around three thicknesses of cord in total). Wrap it four to five times until you have nearly reached the loop you made in Step 2.

continued →

KNOTTING CORD AND RIBBON

Decorative cord and ribbon can contribute to the design. One way to do this is with the use of knots.

USING TWO CORDS OR RIBBONS

If your cord is fine enough, or your bead holes large enough, then using two different-colored or textured cords or ribbons creates a whole new look.

KNOTTING BETWEEN BEADS

Knotting between beads using overhand knots is the easiest way to show off your cord. If necessary, slide the knot into place using a large, blunt needle.

STEP 1
To add extra decoration, you can thread your beads onto two different-colored cords, treating them as one. Your overhand knots will then have two colors swirling through them.

STEP 2
You can alternate the colors of your knots by knotting each cord around the other in turn, so that the knots switch color between the beads.

STEP 4
Thread the cut end of the cord through the loop and pull tight, making sure that your wraps stay neat and even.

STEP 5
Identify the long length of the cord you have just been working on, not the one you are wrapping around. Pull on this to tighten the loop. You can also pull on the cut end of the cord at the same time.

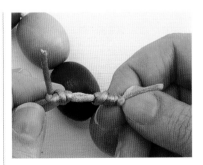

STEP 6
Keep pulling the length of cord and the cut end until the knot and wraps are held tightly around the cords. Repeat on the other cut end of the cord to finish the piece.

With its strength, ease of use, and ability to hold its shape, memory wire is an ingenious jewelry-making tool.

Using memory wire

Memory wire is named for its ability to hold its shape and bounce back from being distorted. Resembling a coiled spring, this stringing material is lightweight, strong, and durable, which means that your jewelry can fit anyone, regardless of size, and can be used without a clasp. Once you know how to choose this versatile material, you can quickly create fun jewelry.

This simple bracelet uses chunky beads in complementary colors for maximum impact.

Memory wire comes in long coils or pre-cut lengths and is sized for use in necklaces, bracelets, or rings. Buying a coil is less expensive and means that you can make items of different lengths. You can find memory wire that is thick and unyielding or finer and more pliable—the choice is yours when making your purchase.

CUTTING MEMORY WIRE

Memory wire is made of toughened steel. As a result, it can easily damage your wire cutters. You can either dedicate one pair of regular wire cutters just to memory wire or purchase a pair of extra-strong cutters designed for the job. Inexpensive hardware-store cutters will do the job perfectly—there is no need to buy expensive jewelry-wire cutters for this.

No matter what cutters you use when you cut memory wire, make sure to hold onto the piece you are removing. Because of the wire's natural springiness, these pieces can easily fly off and hurt someone.

Memory wire coils are available in ring, bracelet, and necklace sizes. Just cut off the length you require.

FINISHING MEMORY WIRE

There are two ways to finish your memory wire jewelry: with turned loops or by gluing on end findings.

TURNED LOOP FINISH

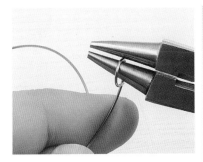

STEP 1
Using a pair of round-nose pliers, grasp the end of your memory wire and make a turned loop. You may find you can't make the loop in one maneuver, so continue until finished.

STEP 2
Thread the beads onto the straight end of the memory wire and trim, using appropriate cutters.

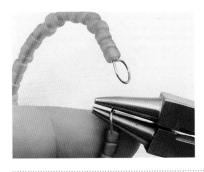

STEP 3
Using the round-nose pliers, make a turned loop at the other end of the wire, matching the size of the first loop.

FINISHING, USING MEMORY WIRE END FINDINGS

STEP 1
Thread your beads and then, using a strong glue, attach a memory wire end finding to one end of the memory wire.

STEP 2
Repeat, adding a memory wire end finding to the other end of your memory wire to finish.

---

4 GREAT REASONS TO USE MEMORY WIRE

- **It's quick and easy to use**—you can create new jewelry in a matter of minutes.

- **It has a one-size-fits-all design.** You can forget about checking sizes if you are making gifts or items to sell.

- **It doesn't need a clasp.** This makes it ideal for anyone who struggles to use a clasp.

- **It uncoils and stretches easily.** Pieces made with memory wire are easy to remove, making it ideal for children's jewelry.

A pretty mixture of faceted glass beads gives this green bracelet plenty of sparkle.

Stringing using crimp beads is a fast, modern alternative to traditional methods that allows you to whip up a piece of jewelry quickly and easily.

Crimping and stringing

The modern alternative to stringing and knotting, crimping has sped up the stringing process so that you can master how to make securely strung jewelry. Once you've learned the basic steps and tricks, you'll be on your way to designing and making beautiful strung jewelry in no time.

This strung turquoise and silver necklace uses crimp covers for a neat finish at the end.

BASIC CRIMPING TECHNIQUE

Crimping involves stringing all your beads onto a nylon-coated steel wire, then using small crimp beads, pressed to bite into the nylon coating, to secure the ends. You can use either flat-nose or specially designed crimping pliers for this technique.

USING FLAT-NOSE PLIERS

Flat-nose pliers simply flatten the crimp.

Place the beading wires inside the crimp and rest the crimp inside the jaws of your pliers. Press down hard to secure.

USING CRIMPING PLIERS

Crimping pliers not only squash your crimp but also round it, giving a neater finish. They have two notches in their jaws to do the job.

Squash the crimp.

STEP 1
Place the beading wires inside the crimp and lay the crimp in the notch nearest the handle in your pliers jaws (the notch is shaped like a figure 8). Press down to squash the crimp.

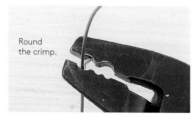

Round the crimp.

STEP 2
Remove your work from the pliers, rotate the flattened crimp so that it sits on its side, and place it in the first notch on your pliers (the rounded notch). Press down to fold your crimp in half and round it.

HIDING YOUR CRIMP

If you don't like the look or sharp edges of your crimp, you can hide it inside a crimp cover.

Place the crimp cover over your crimp bead and press down, using either flat-nose pliers or the rounded notch in your crimping pliers to close and secure the cover.

STRINGING WITH CRIMPS

Once your necklace is designed, you can begin to string it. It doesn't matter if you string it and then finish the ends, just as long as you make sure you don't lose any beads off the ends.

STEP 1
Using a crimp bead, securely attach a length of beading wire to one end of your clasp. Make sure the loop you create is large enough to move easily within the clasp.

STEP 2
Trim the end of the beading wire close to the crimp, but keep it long enough so that there is still a sufficient length of wire to be hidden in your beads.

STEP 3
String on all of the beads, then add another crimp and the other end of your clasp. Make sure your beads haven't slipped and are still covering the beading wire at the other end of your piece before continuing.

STEP 4
Thread the end of your beading wire back through a few beads and pull tight, making only a little loop against your clasp.

STEP 5
Using wire cutters, trim the beading wire close to the bead it is exiting. Very gently expand the loop that the clasp sits in so that the cut end of the wire slides inside the bead it was exiting. Squash the crimp at this end to finish.

4 | GOOD PRACTICES TO FOLLOW

- **Make sure the strands of beading wire are lying side by side.** They should not be crossed over inside the crimp.

- **Check the size of the loop that goes through the clasp.** It should be large enough to move easily and not rub on the clasp and wear.

- **Make sure you hide the cut ends of your beading wire.** They can be sharp—tuck them away inside the beads.

- **Bear in mind that the crimp size and the wire size are related.** With the wrong match, the wire either won't go through the crimp at all or it will slip out even after crimping.

This advanced, traditional technique can be used to make fashion items or heirloom pieces, and gives an elegant and secure finish that will stand the test of time.

Pearl knotting

Pearl stringing and knotting is the name for a traditional stringing technique that applies whether you're stringing tiny beads or large fashion beads. The techniques are designed to use with a fine, soft, flexible stringing material, such as silk or nylon cord, and give you a piece of jewelry that drapes wonderfully when worn. Whether you use the advanced technique or the easier, shortened version, the end result will be worth the work.

The fine thread and pearl knotting make these flat-edged gemstone beads drape and bend nicely. Any other technique would create a rigid necklace.

MAKING A FINE NEEDLE

When working with gemstones and pearls, you will find they have very small holes—so working with a normal needle may be impossible. In addition, the basic thread-and-French-wire method of stringing makes use of a double thread, which is too thick to be worked with a normal needle. Therefore, you'll need to use a needle that's fine enough to pass through the beads and also to be cut off.

STEP 1
Cut a short length of fine wire (30ga/0.2mm or finer) and close the ends together to form a loop around your thread.

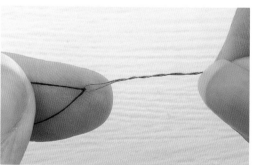

STEP 2
Grasping the cut ends of the wire tightly—using flat-nose pliers if necessary—begin twisting the wire around itself from the loop down until you've made a fine needle. The more you twist it, the neater and finer it will be. Trim the ends before use.

If you want to cheat, stringing tiny seed beads between each pearl will replicate the look of knots.

USING THREAD AND FRENCH WIRE

Using a fine thread paired with French wire (to protect your thread) is an ideal way to create an elegant piece of jewelry. Knotting between each bead is optional with this method.

STEP 1
Cut two lengths of French wire about ½ in (1cm) long. Depending on the size of your clasp, you may need to cut a different length. Make sure your wire is long enough to completely cover any thread that goes through your clasp.

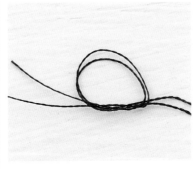

STEP 2
Cut a length of thread double the length you want your finished piece to be (or four times longer if knotting). Add the fine needle you made on page 40. Knot the ends of the threads together.

STEP 3
Thread on one bead and a length of French wire. Thread through the attaching loop in your clasp and then back down your bead. This end will be neatened later, but leave a short length of thread.

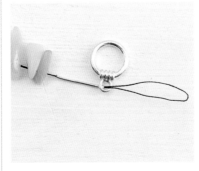

STEP 4
String on all your beads and then the other length of French wire and the other end of your clasp. Remove the fine needle.

continued ⟶

6 | TRICKS FOR SUCCESSFUL KNOTTING

- **Make the first bead hole larger.** When using the traditional French-wire method, the first bead you thread will have four strands of thread through. You may need to make the hole slightly larger with a bead reamer to allow for this.

- **Be prepared for the work to loosen.** Your work may be tight when first strung, but it will soon loosen with wear. To allow for this, you can pull the length through your fingers a few times to stretch the thread before you use it.

- **Use single thread with clamshells.** The methods described here use doubled thread through the beads. When using clamshells (see page 43), you can use single thread instead.

- **Go slow and pay attention.** It's easy—especially toward the end—to lose concentration as you finish knotting a long strand, so if you accidentally find you tighten a knot in the wrong place, it will be very hard to undo with this fine thread.

- **Watch the position of your knots.** Don't let the weight of your beaded strand pull your knots tight in the wrong place when you pull the strand through.

- **Be gentle with your French wire.** Although it is designed to protect your thread, French wire by itself is very fragile and can easily be pulled apart or distorted. It's best to cut it with wire cutters rather than scissors, which may squash the French wire.

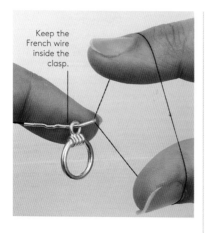

Keep the French wire inside the clasp.

STEP 5
At the second end, slide the clasp and French wire close to the end loop of thread. Insert your fingers through the loop and take hold of the clasp and French wire, making sure that the clasp sits on the French wire.

STEP 6
Pull tight so that the loop of thread catches on the length of thread and the clasp is sitting on the French wire, which is now bent.

A thick needle or awl is perfect for sliding knots.

STEP 7
Slide one bead to the French wire. If you're using knots, tie an overhand knot and position it close to the bead with your needle. If you're not knotting, simply slide all your beads to the French wire and skip the next step.

USING A KNOTTING TOOL

There are a variety of knotting tools on the market. Each one is slightly different, but their general purpose is to help to slide the tied knot close to the beads and to keep the knots uniform.

Knots slide off the awl-shaped prong.

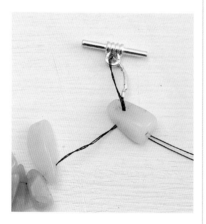

STEP 8
Continue sliding on single beads and then knotting until you have just one bead left. Slide this down but do not tie a knot.

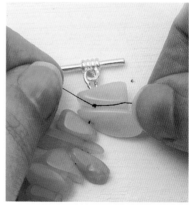

STEP 9
Working carefully, adjust the bead, French wire, and clasp from the starting end so that they slide down close to the rest of the work. Cut off the knot and use the thread ends to tie the string closely between the French wire and the last bead. Trim neatly to finish.

USING CLAMSHELLS

This method gives your strand the look and feel of the more complicated thread-and-French-wire method, but it is quicker and easier to do.

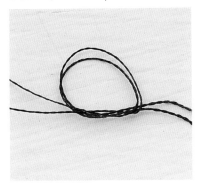

STEP 1
Cut thread more than double the length of the finished piece you want (or four times longer if you're knotting). Add a fine needle and tie the ends together with an overhand knot.

STEP 2
Trim the thread ends and place the knot inside a clamshell. Use flat-nose pliers or the rounded notch of crimping pliers to close the clamshell around the knot.

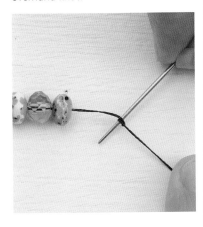

STEP 3
If using knots, string on one bead, then tie an overhand knot after it, using a large needle to slide it close to the bead. Repeat with the remaining beads. If not knotting, simply string all the beads and then tie a knot.

STEP 4
Trim the thread close to the knot, place the knot inside a clamshell, then close as before. Use jump or split rings to attach a clasp to each end.

4. CLEVER WAYS WITH BIG BEAD HOLES

- **Try using a thicker thread.** Rather than a fine thread, a thicker one will fill larger bead holes.

- **Place small beads on either side of your large ones.** This will ensure that the knots stay on each side of the two small beads and won't disappear inside the larger single bead.

- **Push small beads inside larger ones.** This will help fill the larger holes—visually, all you'll see are the large beads.

- **Tie two or more knots on top of each other.** This makes the knots larger and will help to hold the larger beads in place. ·

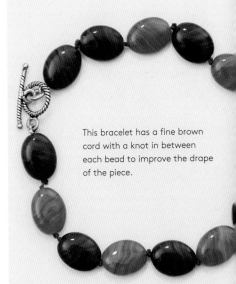

This bracelet has a fine brown cord with a knot in between each bead to improve the drape of the piece.

The only thing better than strung jewelry is more strung jewelry—so learn these basic techniques and tips to create beautiful multi-strand pieces.

Multi-strand jewelry

There are many different ways to create multi-strand jewelry. As you progress with your jewelry making, you may find your own favorite—or even an entirely new method—but these basic techniques and styles will get you started.

MULTI-STRANDS OF CORD

MULTI-STRANDS OF BEADING THREAD

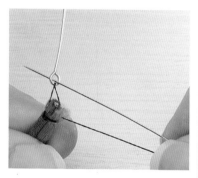

STITCHING ONTO AN EYE PIN
Cord ends can be attached to eye pins and hidden in end cones. Use a needle and thread to stitch thick cords securely onto the loop of an eye pin.

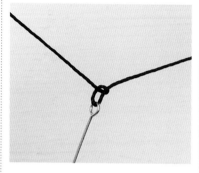

KNOTTING ONTO AN EYE PIN
Knot beading thread onto the eye-pin loop. Tie a double knot and add a drop of glue for extra security.

Trim the thread end short. Slide an end cone onto the eye pin to conceal the knots. Make a wrapped or simple loop above the end cone to attach your findings.

CORD CRIMPS
You may be able to fit two pieces of cord into one cord crimp, or use two of them and a jump ring to join them to your clasp.

CLAMSHELLS
More than one thread knotted together will fit inside a single clamshell.

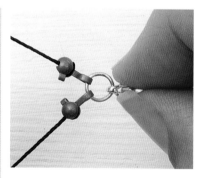

If you make multiple strands, you may need extra clamshells attached to your clasp.

This multi-strand choker uses spacer bars at either end and within the strands to keep the strands separated.

MULTI-STRANDS AND CRIMPING

CRIMPING ONTO AN EYE PIN
Multiple strands of beading wire can be crimped onto an eye pin and then hidden inside an end cone.

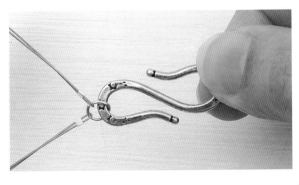

CRIMPING ONTO JUMP RINGS
For interchangeable multi-strands, crimp your beading wire onto jump rings and use an S-hook to fasten.

5 KEY QUESTIONS TO CONSIDER

- **Do you want to hide the ends of your work?** Then end caps are the ideal solution.

- **Are you using cord and want a simpler ending?** Then putting two or more cords in a cord crimp is possible—but if you have more cord lengths, you may need to use more cord findings.

- **Are you using cord and want to hide the ends?** Then stitching the cord to an eye pin and covering it with an end cone will solve the problem.

- **Do you want to keep your multi-strands from overlapping when worn?** Then you will need spacer bars.

- **Do you have too many strands for one eye pin?** Then you can use two or more inside your end cone or make the loop on the eye pin larger.

End cones are ideal for hiding the ends of your strands.

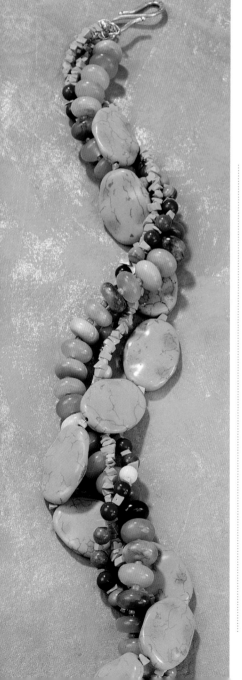

Multi-strand magic

Go from single to multi-strands in no time at all with this interchangeable necklace, designed to be altered at a moment's notice.

MATERIALS AND TOOLS

- Multiple strands of gemstone beads
- Beading wire
- Crimp beads
- Crimp covers (optional)
- Solid jump rings or large jump rings
- S-hook clasp (or the wire to make one)
- Wire cutters
- Flat-nose or crimping pliers

TECHNIQUES See also:

- Crimping and stringing, page 38
- Making your own findings, page 80

MAKING A STRAND

STEP 1

Using a crimp bead and your pliers, secure one end of your beading wire to a jump ring. Trim the wire close to the crimp.

STEP 2

String all the beads for one of your necklace strands, making sure to cover the cut end of the wire. Then thread on a crimp bead and a jump ring.

STEP 3

Thread the cut end of the beading wire back through some of your beads and pull tight, holding it securely against the jump ring. Trim the wire close to the bead it is exiting.

STEP 4
Gently pull on the jump ring to loosen the loop of beading wire around it. Stop when the cut end of the beading wire has pulled inside a bead.

STEP 5
Crush your crimp bead with your pliers and make sure it is secure. If desired, you can now cover both crimp beads with crimp covers to hide them.

STEP 6
Repeat Steps 1–5 to make as many strands of gemstones as desired. Vary the length of some of them for a different look.

STEP 7
To wear the necklace, thread a jump ring over the S-hook clasp.

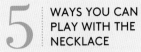

5 WAYS YOU CAN PLAY WITH THE NECKLACE

- **Make strands of different or even graduating lengths.**

- **Look to the color wheel** (see page 16) for guidance on colors. A few strands of one color worn with a strand of a contrasting color—for example, blue with orange, red with green, or yellow with purple—gives a dramatic look.

- **Make your expensive gemstones go further** by spacing them out with seed beads.

- **Extend the drape** by exchanging beading wire for thread and clamshells, simply attaching the clamshells to the jump rings.

- **Add texture** to simpler strands using different-shaped beads.

The design of this necklace means that you can easily mix and match different strands for a whole new look, whenever the mood takes you.

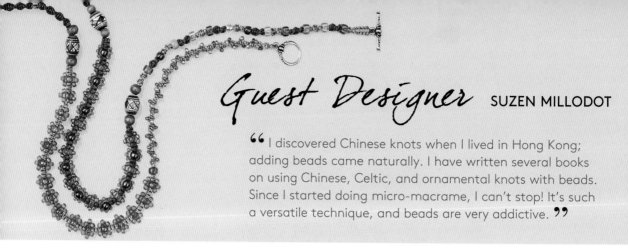

Guest Designer SUZEN MILLODOT

" I discovered Chinese knots when I lived in Hong Kong;
adding beads came naturally. I have written several books
on using Chinese, Celtic, and ornamental knots with beads.
Since I started doing micro-macrame, I can't stop! It's such
a versatile technique, and beads are very addictive. "

Serendipity wrap bracelet

Improvize this bracelet as you go along, using up some of the odd
beads in your collection. The bracelet wraps six times around the wrist,
and it is long enough to wear as a necklace or anklet if preferred.

SQUARE KNOT

STEP 1
Start with a right-hand half knot. Take the right-hand
strand across the center cords and under the left strand. To
complete the first half knot, take the left strand under the
center cords and up over the right strand.

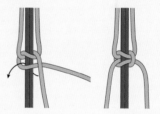

STEP 2
Now make a left-hand half knot. Take the left-hand strand
over the center cords and under the right strand. To
complete the second half knot, take the right-hand strand
under the center cords and over the left strand. The square
knot is now complete.

SPIRAL KNOT—VARIATION ON A SQUARE KNOT

STEP 1
If only the left-hand half knot is
repeated, after every fourth or
fifth knot the knotting will
naturally twist.

STEP 2
Turn the work over and carry on
knotting as before.

TECHNIQUES See also:

Using cord and ribbon, page 32

STEP 1

Cut one piece of red cord 5yd (4.5m) long. Cut another four pieces 3yd (2.75m) long, one in red, one in dark wine color, and two in yellow. Brush clear nail polish on all ten ends and let dry.

MATERIALS AND TOOLS

- C-Lon Tex 400 cord (0.9mm diameter) or Chinese braided knotting cord of the same thickness (0.8 to 1mm) in yellow, red, and wine colors
- A selection of size 8 seed beads in gold, red, topaz, deep pink, and pumpkin-orange.(Toho seed beads have larger holes than other seed beads and so it's easier to thread cords through them.)
- 6mm glass pony beads (they have large holes) in red, gold, turquoise, dark pink, and blue
- A selection of size 6 seed beads in pumpkin-orange and copper
- Decorative beads from your stash, about 8–10mm, with holes large enough to take 4 cords, approximately 2–3mm. Wood beads have large holes, as do pewter, plastic, ceramic, and lampwork beads. I used ceramic beads here.
- Miyuki size 6 triangular seed beads in blue and light blue (Toho size 6 cube-shaped seed beads could also be used)
- Flower-shaped beads (or similar) with 2mm holes
- Attractive toggle clasp
- Tape measure
- Sharp scissors
- Clear nail polish to stiffen the ends of the cords for threading
- Macrame knotting board
- Dressmaker's pins with colored spherical tops
- Instant glue gel
- Thread burner (optional)

STEP 2

Pin half of the toggle clasp to the macrame knotting board. Thread the 5yd (4.5m) length of red cord and the 3yd (2.75m) golden yellow cord through the toggle clasp until they fall halfway.

STEP 3

The longer red cord doubled becomes your center cords. Using the yellow cords, referring to the knot diagrams, tie six half knots, starting with the right-hand cord on top. You have made spiral knots. Turn the knotting over when it wants to twist.

STEP 4

Thread one size 8 gold-color seed bead onto the right-hand cord and make a half knot.

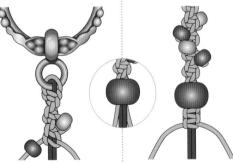

STEP 5

Make another unbeaded half knot. Thread one size 8 red seed bead onto the left-hand cord and make another right-hand half knot. Make another unbeaded half knot. Continue in this way for approximately 5 in (13cm).

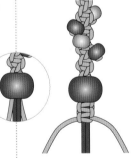

STEP 6

Thread all four cords through one 6mm red glass pony bead. Referring to the knot diagrams, make two square knots underneath the 6mm pony bead.

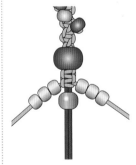

STEP 7

Thread three size 8 topaz seed beads onto the cords on each side. Thread one size 6 pumpkin-orange seed bead onto the central doubled red cords.

STEP 8
Make three square knots underneath the central bead. Push your new square knots upward to form a six-petaled flower shape.

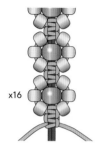

STEP 9
Continue making the flower shapes with three square knots in between until you have 16 flower shapes. Finish with three square knots.

x16

STEP 10
Now it is time to change to a new colored knotting cord. Here's how: thread all four cords through a red 6mm glass pony bead. Then choose a decorative bead from your collection that is about 8 to 10mm long, with a hole large enough for all four cords. This will be threaded on after the next step.

STEP 11
Trim the ends only of the yellow knotting cords so that they will be hidden under the bead. Put a spot of nail polish onto the ends so that they will adhere to the center cords and stay in place. Thread on the large bead from Step 10 to cover the ends of the glued-down cords. Add another red 6mm glass pony bead.

STEP 12
With the exact center of the new wine-colored cord placed underneath the red central cords, make 16 right-hand half knots until the spiral knotting is 1 in (25mm) long. Thread all four cords through one size 6 blue Miyuki triangular seed bead.

STEP 13
Make about 16 left-hand half knots (they will twist in the opposite direction), then add a light blue triangle bead as before.

STEP 14
Continue in this way, alternating the direction of knotting between beads, until the knotting is about 7 in (18cm) long. Thread all four cords through a gold-color 6mm pony bead. Thread on a large rondelle bead sideways, as shown, with two cords going upward and two downward.

STEP 15
Thread all four cords through another 6mm pony bead, then add another rondelle bead sideways like the first one. Thread all four cords through a 6mm pony bead. The picture shows how the cords are threaded. When worn, they will lie flat on the wrist.

STEP 16
Make eight right-hand half knots. Add one size 8 deep pink seed bead onto the right side only, then make another half knot, followed by an unbeaded half knot. Continue adding a bead to every alternate right-hand half knot until the knotted section is 3 in (7cm) long.

STEP 17
Thread a pink flower bead onto all four cords. Make six half knots, then add a second pink flower bead. Make six more half knots and add a third pink flower bead.

STEP 18
Repeat Step 16 until you have another 3 in (7cm) of spiral knots and size 8 deep pink seed beads, as in Step 16. Then add three turquoise-blue flower beads in exactly the same way as you did with the pink beads in Step 17. Make another 3 in (7cm) of spiral knots and size 8 seed beads.

STEP 19

The dark wine-colored cords are now coming to an end, so you will need to add the red knotting cords that you have already cut and prepared. As you did in Steps 10 and 11, thread all four cords through a 6mm pony bead—this time in turquoise—then hide the trimmed ends of the wine-colored cord under a larger bead. Add another turquoise 6mm round pony bead underneath.

x18

STEP 20

Add the red knotting cord, make two square knots, and follow Steps 7, 8, and 9 to make 18 flower shapes, alternating size 8 pumpkin-orange beads with size 6 copper-colored beads, and size 8 topaz seed beads with size 6 pumpkin-orange beads. Make two square knots to finish.

FINISHED SIZE
49 in (125cm) long, including clasp

STEP 21

Change to the yellow cord. As you did in Steps 10 and 11, thread all four cords through a round red wood bead (or pony bead), then trim the shortest red cords, glue them to the central cords, and slip the large bead over to hide them. Add another round red bead. Start knotting with the new yellow cord, as you did in Steps 12 and 19. Make nine half knots with the yellow cord.

STEP 22

Thread one 6mm dark pink pony bead onto all four cords. Below this, swap the knotting cords and the center cords so that you are knotting the red cord around the yellow cord. Change the direction of the twist each time.

STEP 23

Make nine half knots, then thread one 6mm blue pony bead onto all four cords. Swap the knotting cords and center cords again and make nine half knots. Continue in this way until you have 6 in (15cm) of knotting.

STEP 24

Thread the center cords through the other half of the toggle, 1 in (2.5cm) below the knotting, as shown. Trim the ends of the folded center cords to 1 in (2.5 cm) long.

STEP 25

Glue the trimmed cord ends down and continue with square knots over the folded cords until you reach the toggle. Glue and trim the cord ends neatly.

Guest Designer

LYNN DAVY

" I am a bead artist based in the UK, best known for my colorful seed bead jewelry. I love texture, randomness, and getting other people enthused about beads. "

Knotted pearl necklace

FINISHED SIZE
15 in (38cm) long, including clasp

MATERIALS AND TOOLS

- 1 x 6 ft 6 in (2m) strand each of bright red, turquoise, and dark red #5 Griffin silk cord with wire needle
- 30 x metallic bronze Japanese 2mm cube beads
- 61 x bronze chocolate baroque 6–6.5mm freshwater pearls
- 3 in (6cm) sterling-silver French wire, cut into ½ in (1cm) lengths
- 8 x copper 4mm jump rings
- 10 x rich brown baroque 5–6mm freshwater pearls
- 51 x mulberry baroque 6–6.5mm freshwater pearls
- 11 x rainbow moonstone 4mm round beads
- 2 x copper 3-to-1 links
- 1 x copper two-part hook-and-eye clasp (or clasp of your choice)
- Sharp scissors
- Wire cutters
- Pearl knotting tool (or tweezers and awl)
- E-6000 glue or clear nail polish
- Two pairs flat-nose pliers

A fun variation on the classic pearl-knotting technique, this three-stranded design makes a feature of the knots by using colored silk.

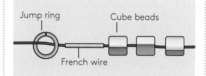

Jump ring   Cube beads

French wire

STEP 1: STARTING EACH STRAND

Unwind all of the bright red silk from the card. Stretch the silk between your hands to remove the worst of the kinks. String three metallic bronze cube beads, a piece of French wire, and a copper jump ring. Pull all but 2 in (5cm) of the silk right through them, so that they are near the tail end.

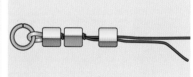

STEP 2

Pass the needle back through the third cube (the one nearest the French wire). Pull the silk through carefully until the French wire forms a horseshoe shape. Knot the long end of the silk (the part with the needle attached) together with the thread just after the cube. Go through the next cube and make another knot. Go through the third cube, make a third knot, and pull it as tight as you can. Do not trim the short end yet.

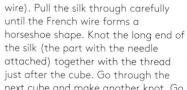

TECHNIQUES See also:

Pearl knotting, page 40
Opening and closing jump rings, page 64

STEP 3: INNER STRAND

Now string the beads for the first (shortest) strand as follows: two bronze pearls, one cube, two bronze pearls, one brown pearl, two bronze pearls, one brown pearl. Repeat five times, finishing with an additional two bronze pearls.

STEP 4: KNOT AND FINISH

Slide the first pearl close to the last knot that you tied. Use your knotting tool to tie a knot after the pearl. Continue to slide beads up to the start of the thread, knotting between each one. After the last pearl, don't tie a knot. Add three cubes, a piece of French wire and a jump ring. Pass the needle back through the last cube and tie a knot. Then go back through the second and third cubes, tying a knot each time. Leave about 2 in (5cm) and cut the thread.

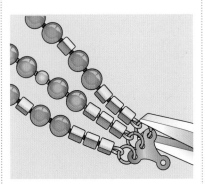

BEADER'S WISDOM

• • •

Time spent beading is never wasted. You learn from each and every piece, even if what you learn is that you need to do it differently next time. Beads are easy to recycle, and thread is relatively inexpensive, so don't be afraid to experiment.

INNER STRAND

2 bronze pearls   2 bronze pearls   2 bronze pearls

1 cube   1 brown pearl   1 brown pearl

MIDDLE STRAND

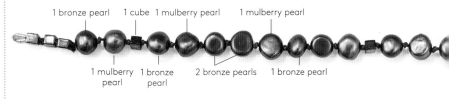

2 mulberry pearls   2 mulberry pearls   2 mulberry pearls

1 moonstone   1 moonstone   1 cube

OUTER STRAND

1 bronze pearl   1 cube   1 mulberry pearl   1 mulberry pearl

1 mulberry pearl   1 bronze pearl   2 bronze pearls   1 bronze pearl

STEP 5: MIDDLE STRAND

Repeat Steps 1 and 2 with the turquoise silk. String: two mulberry pearls, one moonstone, two mulberry pearls, one moonstone, two mulberry pearls, one cube. Repeat five times, plus the first five beads of the sequence. Repeat Step 4 to knot and finish.

STEP 6: OUTER STRAND

Repeat Steps 1 and 2 with the dark red silk. String one bronze pearl, one mulberry pearl, one cube, one bronze pearl, one mulberry pearl, two bronze pearls, one mulberry pearl, one bronze pearl. Repeat five times plus the first five beads of the sequence. Repeat Step 4 to knot and finish.

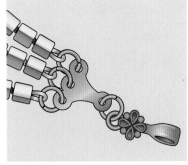

STEP 7: ASSEMBLY

Add a tiny drop of glue to the final knot on each strand. Allow the glue to dry completely, preferably overnight, then trim the ends of the threads. Use jump rings and pliers to attach the strands to the links.

STEP 8: CLASP

Use jump rings to attach one half of the clasp to each end of the necklace.

CHAPTER 3

Wirework

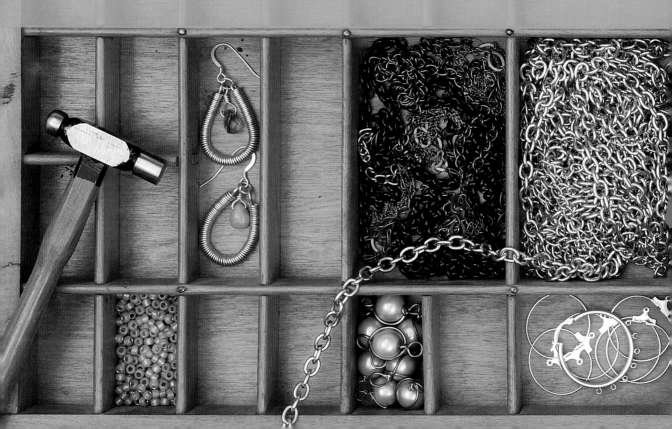

A few easy techniques are all you need to begin creating jewelry with beads and wire. Discover how to make loops, coils, chains, and to even create your own findings. Whether your style is simple or elaborate, there's a technique to suit and a project to inspire.

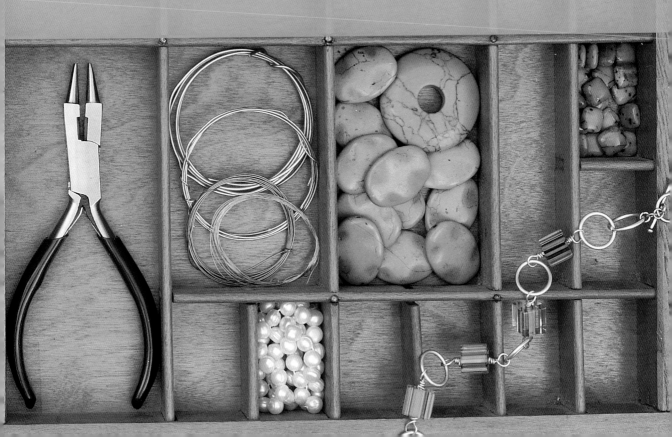

1

2

3

4

Wirework:
be inspired

1. LYNDA CARSON The blackened oxydized copper wire that wraps around the faceted blue glass beads (right) and lavender lampwork beads (left) adds a rustic charm to these briolette earrings, which is enhanced with the artisan-made earwires.

2. DEBBIE POYSER The rich contrasts of the colors and textures in this design are a great success. The long pendant features a Swarovski teardrop pearl intricately wrapped in 70 in (180cm) of fine, gold-fill wire. A gold chain with hammered links gives a glamorous finish.

3. ELEONORA PERLIC Eleonora hand formed, wire-wrapped, and lightly hammered the copper wire to create this cuff. The metal was "painted" with a flame to achieve its vibrant, fiery color. The cuff is embellished with 18 x ⅛ in (4mm) round turquoise stones.

4. LINDA JONES This unusual necklace combines hammered bronze and silver wire in a floral centerpiece, complemented with asymmetric strands of amethyst chips and a bronze toggle clasp.

5. LINDA JONES Silver wire is shaped and hammered into repeating teardrop components. These components are linked with jump rings and adorned with faceted glass bead dangles, to create a bib necklace that is bold yet delicate.

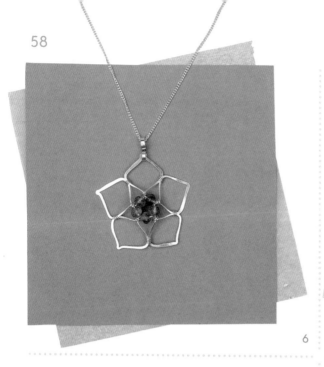

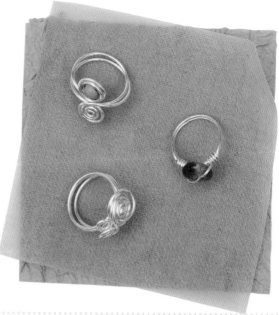

6

7

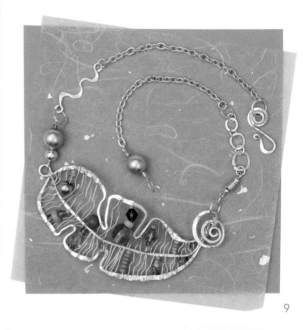

8

9

6. KRISTIN SMITH This simple, five-bead flower pendant is made from soft round silver wire and 4–5mm lavender rondelle beads. The petals are shaped, hammered, and wire-wrapped at the point where each petal meets.

7. LYNDA CARSON These three wire-wrapped rings are made with 18 and 20 gauge anti-tarnish silver craft wire. The lower ring shows how

wire can be manipulated to provide a focal point, whereas the rings above feature a recycled glass disc and a round turquoise bead.

8. DEBBIE POYSER Debbie has used two gauges of copper wire and a sturdy wire frame to construct the leaf-shaped pendant for this bracelet. While wire-wrapping the outer edge of the leaf, the finer-wire veins were intermittently woven

within the frame. Wire-wrapped, Japanese glass Miyuki beads embellish the chain.

9. LINDA JONES Hammered wire has been formed into a sinuous freeform shape and wrapped with finer wire and an assortment of glass beads to make the striking focal piece for this necklace. Wire coils and a handmade clasp complete the pleasing asymmetric design.

10

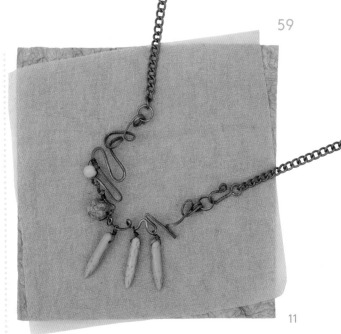

11

12

13

10. HUAN PHAM Swarovski crystal pearls are woven together with silver wire to create the intricate components that form the centerpiece of this opulent necklace. The elegantly curved wire ends give a sensation of movement and delicacy to the design.

11. ELEONORA PERLIC This asymmetric pendant is hand formed from copper wire. The position and combination of the five turquoise beads creates additional interest.

12. ABBY HOOK Inspired by the twisted wire torcs made by the Iceni tribe, Abby's bracelet achieves the same look of strength combined with simple, delicate detail. Made with 6-loop double Viking knit chain, the bracelet is finished with handmade wire caps, and accented with turquoise beads.

13. DEBBIE POYSER Wire-wrapping and weaving techniques were used to create this elegant gold-filled bracelet. The flower motif was hand formed and the center woven with fine-gauge, gold-filled wire. The wire-wrapped edging incorporates tiny gray labradorite beads.

Wirework is all about manipulating and showcasing wire to create jewelry, and these essential materials and tools are what you will need to make beautiful pieces.

Essential wirework tools and supplies

1 ROUND-NOSE PLIERS
Round-nose pliers are perfect for making loops in wire.

2 FLAT-NOSE PLIERS
Flat-nose or chain-nose pliers are used to make sharp bends or to hold your wire as you work. The difference between the two is that the jaws of flat-nose pliers are the same width all the way along, while chain-nose pliers taper toward the end. Whenever the instructions refer to flat-nose pliers, you can use either type.

3 THREE-STEP PLIERS
These are similar to round-nose pliers, but one of the jaws has three different-sized steps on it, which are great for helping you make the same-sized loop or tube.

4 CRIMPING PLIERS
The rounded notch on these is perfect for pressing over the cut wire end when you've finished making a wrapped loop. Not only does this press the wire into the component, but it gently rounds it, too.

5 CUTTERS
You can buy end or flush (side) cutters and their name reflects where their blades sit.

6 MEASURING TOOLS
Rulers or tape measures are essential to help you make neat components that are all the same size.

7 FILES
To remove sharp edges and burrs, it is essential to file your wire. You can purchase files made just for this, or even use emery boards or nail files. If you want to round the ends of your wire perfectly, then burr cups or wire rounders are the tools you need.

8 MANDRELS
If you want to make loops in your wirework and find that your round-nose pliers aren't wide or long enough, then you can use other forms such as wooden dowels, metal rods, and even the barrels of pens to help you get the shape that you want.

9 HAMMER AND BLOCK
You'll need a suitable hammer and block when you want to enter the world of texturing or hardening your wire and components. To make noticeable marks, a metal hammer and block are perfect. For hardening but not marking, wood or soft plastic are ideal. A ball-peen hammer has one rounded and one flat end, and is great for giving you more options.

10 WIRE
Available as round, semi-round, oval, and even square, wire is a great material with which to make jewelry due to its availability, ease of use, color choices, and strength. Wire is sold either by gauge (ga) or by mm, both of which are referred to as diameter. The gauge most commonly used is American Wire Gauge (AWG), and although the two measurements don't match up exactly, a rough conversion is usually close enough for most wirework.

11 WALLPAPER SCRAPER
If the component you're hammering has a bead on it, you can use a scraper to guard the bead and help guide the hammer to where you want it. Simply place it between the bead and the point where you want to hammer.

12 MASKING/DECORATOR'S TAPE
This is great for marking your pliers, holding coils of wire, identifying wire size, and softening the jaws of your flat-nose pliers if you're worried about marking your tape or holding components together while working.

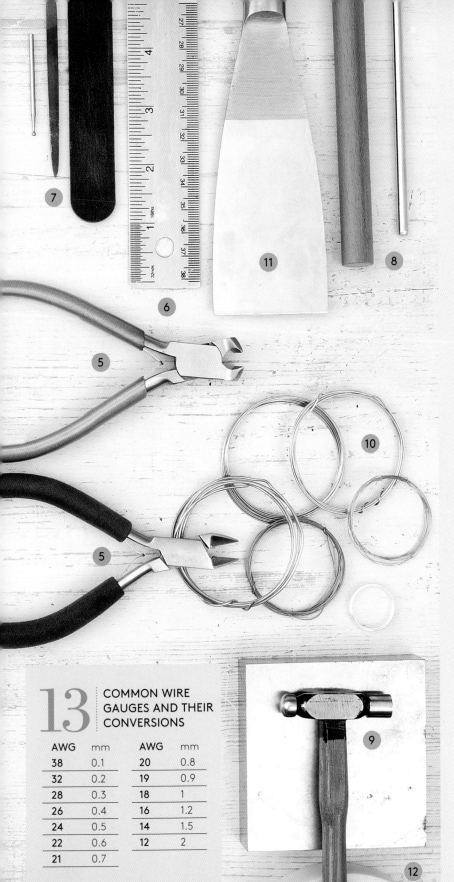

6 QUESTIONS TO HELP YOU CHOOSE THE RIGHT WIRE

- **Do you need strength?** If so, then a size such as 20ga/0.8mm or thicker is perfect.

- **Are your bead holes small?** Many gemstones have small holes, so you may need to use 22ga/0.6mm or finer wire.

- **Is it for weaving around?** The thicker the wire, the harder it is to work and move around easily, so if you plan on wrapping fine wire to decorate a component, you may want to use 26ga/0.4mm or finer.

- **Are you making a clasp?** For security, thicker wire is better, as it is stronger and less likely to come undone or bend. So when making clasps such as S-hooks choose 20ga/0.8mm or thicker.

- **Do you want a dramatic look?** If so, the thicker the wire, the more it will stand out. A diameter of 14ga/1.5mm or more is great, but beware—it will be a lot harder to work with.

- **Are you making earring findings?** These need to be fine enough to go through the holes in ears, so 20–24ga/0.8–0.5mm wire or finer is ideal for findings.

13 COMMON WIRE GAUGES AND THEIR CONVERSIONS

AWG	mm	AWG	mm
38	0.1	20	0.8
32	0.2	19	0.9
28	0.3	18	1
26	0.4	16	1.2
24	0.5	14	1.5
22	0.6	12	2
21	0.7		

The first step in turning a length of wire into a piece of wonderful jewelry is learning how to cut it safely, economically, and accurately.

Measuring, cutting, and filing

Learning the basics of using wire will give you the background to safely create beautiful jewelry that will be admired by all. Put your knowledge of wirework to the test—and explore your creativity!

There are two main types of wire cutters, which are named for the position of their blades: side and end cutters. Although each one is used in the same way, they each have pros and cons.

End cutters: These can handle much thicker wire but, because of their shape, you might find it tricky to get close to the exact cutting point.

Side cutters: The blades of these cutters are generally better for finer wire (18ga/1mm or less), and their points will enable you to get closer to the point where you want to cut. Using the flat side of the blade against the wire you want to retain will allow you to make a neater, flatter cut and to work more closely.

MEASURING AND CUTTING WIRE

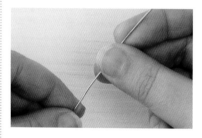

STEP 1

Gently unwind your wire from its coil or reel. As you do so, run it through your fingers to straighten it. This will help to make an accurate cut to the size you want. It also removes some of the spring from the wire, making it easier to work with.

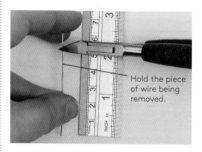

Hold the piece of wire being removed.

STEP 2

Bring your wire to your ruler or measuring tape. Using your wire cutters, carefully cut the length you need, making sure that your fingers are out of the way of the blades and that you are prepared to catch the wire if it flies away.

5 SAFETY TIPS TO CONSIDER WHEN CUTTING WIRE

- **Straightening the wire before you cut it makes it less springy.** The section you are removing and the section you are keeping will be less likely to spring out and hit you.

- **Always keep your fingers and thumbs away from the cutting blades.**

- **When avoiding the cutting blades, make sure that your fingers don't get caught in the cutter's hinges!**

- **Whenever possible, hold onto both the wire you are keeping and the wire you're removing.** The piece you're removing won't then be able to fly off.

- **If possible, point your wire down and away from you.** You can't always stop it from flying away, but by doing this it will be less likely to hit you or anyone else.

The multiple components in this sparkling bracelet required accurate measuring and cutting to ensure that they fit properly together.

4 WAYS TO GET MORE BANG FOR YOUR BUCK

- **Consider using a cheaper wire,** such as copper, to make both your samples and finished pieces of jewelry.

- **Keep all your scraps,** either to be recycled or traded for cash or credit from your wire supplier. Or pick through your pile when you need just a small piece.

- **When cutting your wire, always cut more than you need.** If you think you need 2 in (5cm), cutting 3 in (8cm) may give you a small amount of wasted wire, but cutting 5 in (13cm) gives you a 3 in (8cm) piece that is big enough to use later.

- **Work directly from your reel or coil of wire** when you can. For example, you can thread your bead onto the reel and then make one end of your simple loop right on the end of the wire so that no wire is cut or wasted.

FILING WIRE

WHAT TO AIM FOR

Whatever tool you use for the job, you want to ensure that the ends of your wire are smooth, have no sharp edges or burrs, and, if necessary, are nicely rounded.

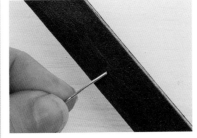

USING AN EMERY BOARD

An emery board is perfect for filing small amounts and getting rid of sharp edges and burrs.

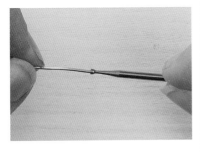

USING A CUP BURR

Also known as wire rounders, these are ideal for rounding the ends of your wire. They can be hand held or placed in an electric drill. Make sure you choose the right size for the wire you're using.

USING A FILE

Using a wire or metal file that's specifically designed for this job will give you a great finish. You can find files with different tooth configurations that will give you different finishes and levels of smoothness.

Wire is a very versatile material to work with. When creating jewelry, you'll need to know how to bend, form, loop, and adjust it to create the components and finished pieces you desire.

Working with wire

Wire lends itself to jewelry making because of its appearance, strength, and ease of use. Before attempting the other techniques in this book, it is essential to learn how to control wire. Once you have mastered holding, folding, and opening your wire and components, your creative journey can proceed.

HOLDING WIRE	BENDING AND FORMING WIRE	OPENING AND CLOSING JUMP RINGS

HOLDING WIRE

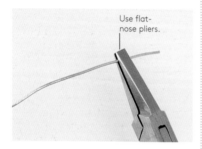

Use flat-nose pliers.

STEP 1

Despite its appearance, wire is quite soft and easily marked. To prevent this and to give you a much better grip on your work, always use flat-nose pliers to hold your wire. This spreads the pressure, grips the wire better, and avoids making dents.

STEP 2

When forming or working on your wire, always hold it as close to the action as possible. This gives you much better control of what you're doing and stops the wire from bending in ways you don't want it to.

BENDING AND FORMING WIRE

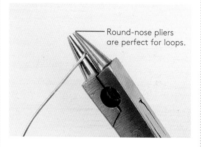

Round-nose pliers are perfect for loops.

STEP 1

Before starting to bend your wire, you must choose the right tool for the job. Round-nose pliers will give you loops and curves, while flat- or chain-nose pliers will give you angles and steps.

Fingers and thumbs do the work.

STEP 2

Although you're using a tool, it is often your fingers that are forming and shaping the wire. By working closely and pressing the wire onto the pliers, you're allowing the wire to take the shape of the form.

OPENING AND CLOSING JUMP RINGS

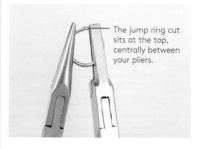

The jump ring cut sits at the top, centrally between your pliers.

STEP 1

Using two pairs of flat-nose pliers, hold the jump ring on either side of the "cut." The pliers should cover as much of the ring as possible to give you a better grip and more control.

Create a gap to fit whatever you're threading through.

STEP 2

Gently pull your dominant hand toward you to open the jump ring. You need to open it just enough to thread on whatever it is you're attaching.

This eye-catching brooch features beautiful beads strung onto copper wire that is bent not only to create the winding shape but also to hold the beads in place. Every curve in this piece—even those used in the catch— were formed around round-nose pliers or larger forms such as a pen barrel.

4 DOS AND DON'TS FOR OPENING AND CLOSING RINGS

- **Never open a ring by pulling the cut ends out to the sides and away from each other.** This makes it lose its loop shape and flattens the side opposite the cut.

- **If one end of your jump ring protrudes above the other,** simply place it inside your pliers and push down to correct.

- **Never pull your non-dominant hand back when opening jump rings.** This will make the ring more awkward for you to thread components onto, especially if you are picking them up directly from your bead mat with the jump ring.

- **Never open your jump ring more than necessary**—it will take a lot more work to close it and could make it lose its shape. Remember that even small extra movements slow you down, cause more work, distort your work, and create unnecessary wear and tear on both your wire and your body!

STEP 3
Attach the required component. Pushing your dominant hand forward, gently close the ring, getting the ends together as much as possible.

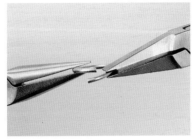

STEP 5
Now push and pull so that the ends cross each other and swap position. This action hardens the metal and ensures a tighter closure in the finished piece.

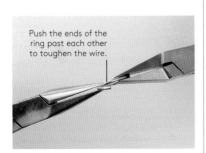

Push the ends of the ring past each other to toughen the wire.

STEP 4
To fully close the ring and make it secure and strong, push your dominant hand slightly forward. Then push both hands together, squeezing the ends of the ring past each other as though you are squashing it.

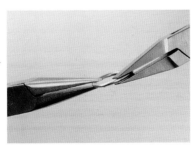

STEP 6
Gently bring the ends of the ring back together and adjust if needed. The pushing and pulling will have toughened the metal and made the ends want to push tightly against each other.

OPENING AND CLOSING OTHER RINGS AND LOOPS

All rings and loops are closed in the same manner as jump rings, but you may find that you can't use two pairs of pliers to do so. Instead, hold the piece in one hand and a pair of pliers in the other and work gently to ensure that the piece is neatly and securely closed.

This delicate necklace demonstrates how you can create a piece of jewelry from just a few beads. It uses lengths of fine silver chain joined with beads on wrapped loops for added length.

Chain, whether made by you or ready-made, is a great way to add a certain look and texture to your jewelry. It can also increase length, create space, and provide a form to decorate.

Using chain

There are so many benefits to using metal chain in wirework. Learning how and when to use it will add to your skills repertoire and range of finished items. Whether the chain has purely visual impact or performs an important structural role, the techniques for working with it are the same, giving you the basis on which to build your creative ideas.

Start by deciding what the chain will be used for. This will govern its look and size. For example, decide whether you want it to be an important visual component or a bold color, larger loop size rather than a small and delicate one.

MEASURING AND CUTTING CHAIN

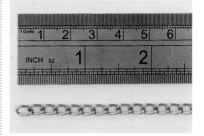

STEP 1
Chain can be measured both by length —inches or centimeters—or by the number of loops. Whichever you choose is up to you, but measuring will save you a lot of time.

Use the previously cut length of chain to help you cut other pieces to match.

STEP 2
If you're going to cut lots of similar lengths, it can help to thread the first cut length onto a piece of wire, then the rest of the chain. Use the cut length as your measure and cut the second piece the same length.

Chain ranges in style from delicate to chunky and comes in many different metal colors and finishes. Choose the one that's right for your project.

This bracelet uses a large silver loop chain as a base on which to hang decorative beads.

4 QUESTIONS TO ASK YOURSELF WHEN CHOOSING CHAIN

- **What color do you want?** Do you want it to coordinate or contrast with your beads?

- **What size loops do you want?** Will you want to thread into the loops, have them stand out, or be more subtle?

- **What thickness of wire do you want the loops made of?** Do you want a heavier chain with more physical and visual impact or something more delicate?

- **Do you need strength?** Then a purchased chain with its soldered links (which won't come apart when you pull on them) is ideal.

DECORATING CHAIN WITH WIRE

STEP 1
Wirework components, in a coordinating material, can be hung from a chain to dress it up. Begin by threading the end of your already-begun component through the appropriate link on the chain.

STEP 2
Finish making the component using either a simple or a wrapped loop, ensuring that it is securely held but able to move freely. Continue adding components until you have the desired design.

DECORATING CHAIN WITH STRINGING

Metal chain can be decorated with beading wire, either unadorned or covered in smaller beads. Simply begin by crimping the wire to the chain links, then weave it through to add color and texture.

STEP 3
If you want some extra help when decorating the chain—or want to see the overall effect as you work—then use a specially designed chain clamp to hold the chain while you work.

Simple loops are the first step in making wirework components and jewelry. All other wirework is built on this technique.

Simple loops

Simple loops are both the physical basis of much wirework jewelry and also the technical basis of most other techniques. Master these few steps, as well as the tips presented here, and soon you'll be on your way to creating wonderful pieces of jewelry that look so much more impressive than the sum of their simple parts.

WITHOUT A BEAD

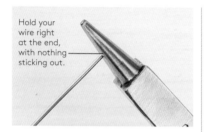

Hold your wire right at the end, with nothing sticking out.

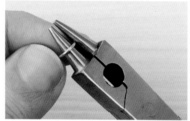

Crimp where the end of the loop wire touches the main strand.

STEP 1
This loop-making method works with no bead on the wire, or one on the reel/coil but out of your way. Begin by grasping your wire at the very end, using the appropriate part of your round-nose pliers for the size of loop that you want to create.

STEP 2
Holding your work closely and using your fingers to form the loop, turn the pliers either away from or toward you. Once you have turned as far as you can, remove the pliers, rotate them to straighten, and reinsert to continue turning.

STEP 3
When the wire touches itself, you'll have a "P"-shaped loop that needs centering. Place the points of your pliers, one inside the loop and the other just under the loop, and "crimp" or bend the wire. Don't worry about adjusting or finessing at this point.

WITH A BEAD

Bend the wire directly above the bead.

Don't undo the right-angle bend you made previously!

STEP 1
This method is used when there's a bead on the wire. Begin by holding the bead tightly above the loop (or end of the wire that's already there), then bend the wire above the bead at a right angle. The more accurate the angle, the better the end result.

STEP 2
Safely trim the wire, leaving 1 in/2.5cm (it can always be trimmed later). Turn the wire so that the point is facing away from you and grasp the end with the appropriate part of your round-nose pliers for the ideal size loop.

STEP 3
Begin to turn a loop. If necessary, reposition the pliers until you make a full loop, making sure you are just forming a loop at the end of the wire and not pulling so hard that you're undoing the right-angle bend.

This spiky necklace has approximately 1,000 head pins, each with a simple loop on the end, which are then all threaded onto beading wire.

STEP 4
Slide a bead into place so that it's set tightly above the loop. Gauge by eye whether the loop is sitting centrally. If necessary, adjust it with pliers or your fingers.

STEP 4
If you have another loop on the same component, compare it to this new one. If either one is too big, you can trim the wire and restart. You can also leave it, as it will look different once attached to something else.

CLINIC ⊕ HOW TO ACHIEVE THE PERFECT SIMPLE LOOP, AND AVOID THE PITFALLS OF MANY BEGINNERS

- **Though loops are one of the simplest wirework techniques, they're one of the trickiest to perfect.** Their simplicity means any flaws can stand out (even if just in your eyes) and their function as an attaching mechanism means that they need to work perfectly or your jewelry may fall apart, or scratch you or your clothes.

- **One of the most common mistakes is not holding the work close enough to where the loop is being made,** resulting in less control over your work. Other mistakes include not grasping the end of the wire (so that some of the wire remains straight); using too much wire (resulting in either different-sized or misshapen loops); using different parts of the pliers (resulting in different-sized loops, but three-step pliers can help); and not closing the loop fully (resulting in the loop separating from what it's attached to or catching on the wearer or their clothes).

- **The top mistake I see? Worrying too much about loops!** For all of your wirework, you're examining it very closely when making it—but the wearer or admirer will be looking at the total effect and overall design, not at the individual loops or differences in size. Also remember that loops look different when joined together or to something else, so don't judge them when they are lying flat and separate.

- **Mastering a technique takes time and everyone makes their own loop sizes and shapes.** With practice, you'll come to know which part of the pliers works best for you, how to do the technique without having to think through every stage, and how much wire to cut off.

Using wrapped loops transforms ordinary beads into designer-style jewelry.

Wrapped loops take a structural technique and dress it up with decorative elements for a whole new look that adds not only security but also extra pizzazz!

Wrapped loops

From the simplicity of simple loops comes the more elaborate technique of wrapped ones. Because these loops cannot be pulled undone, this is a more secure design. It's also more ornamental, with its integral wraps adding texture and visual interest. Although it's tricky at first, you will soon become proficient at it by following the steps below. With practice, you'll come to find this technique indispensable.

MAKING A WRAPPED LOOP

Don't leave a gap between the bead and the base.

STEP 1
Thread the bead onto a head or eye-pin with at least 1½ in/4cm of wire above the bead. Press the bead tight against the base of the wire to ensure that it won't wobble around when finished, and hold securely.

STEP 2
Where you bend the wire determines how many wraps of wire you can fit in. So, as you grip the wire with your flat-nose pliers, think about the distance between the bead and the top of the pliers.

STEP 3
Using your fingers, press the wire above the pliers so that it bends at a right angle. The neater and more accurate the bend, the neater and straighter the wraps (and the better the end result) will be.

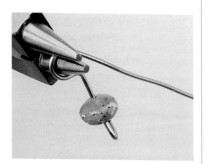

STEP 4
With round-nose pliers, grasp the wire on the bend, using the appropriate part of the pliers for the size of loop you want to make. Grasp the end of the wire with flat-nose pliers and begin pulling it around them to form a loop.

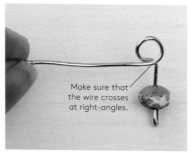

Make sure that the wire crosses at right-angles.

STEP 5
Continue bending the wire until it crosses itself at a right angle. As you do this, the pliers might get in the way, so adjust your hold and keep going.

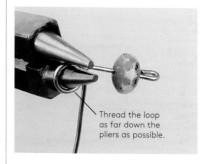

Thread the loop as far down the pliers as possible.

STEP 6
To continue, hold the loop either tightly inside flat-nose pliers or threaded onto round-nose pliers. If doing the latter, make sure that the loop is pressed down as far as it will go so that it doesn't wobble or distort as you continue.

Wrapped loops add extra security to this necklace with large, colorful, heavy beads.

6 MISTAKES BEGINNERS MAKE, AND THEIR CONSEQUENCES

- **Making the bend too far above the bead,** in an attempt to create too many wraps. Keep the bend close to the bead so that the whole piece doesn't become messy and wobbly.

- **Making poor right angles** so that the loop lies at a slant or wraps at an angle and is not straight.

- **Trying to use your hands instead of pliers,** which gives a weak grip on the wire and leads to messy results.

- **Using too little or too much wire,** resulting either in running out of wire before the work is finished or in producing a sloppily finished piece.

- **Not holding the loop securely on the round-nose pliers when wrapping,** so that the whole piece moves around, making it more difficult to continue and resulting in a less neat finished piece. It can also distort the loop.

- **Not being careful with the wrapping,** resulting in wraps overlapping each other or having gaps in between. However, if that's the look you want, then you can ignore this tip!

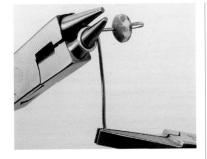

STEP 7
Grasping the end of the wire in flat-nose pliers, wrap it around the small section of wire that sits between the bead and the loop.

STEP 8
Continue forming the wraps until you reach all the way to the top of the bead. You want the wraps to lie exactly next to each other, so take it slowly and concentrate.

STEP 9
Using wire cutters, trim the excess wire as close to the end of the wrapping and the bead as possible. Using pliers, press the cut end tightly into the piece. With their rounded notch, crimping pliers are best for this.

Top: Continue the wraps around the top half of the bead to give the effect of a bead cap.
Bottom: Make a couple of wraps around the top of the bead, then swirl the wire all the way to the other end. Make a couple of wraps at the bottom before finishing with a simple loop.

continued ⟶

JOINING WRAPPED LOOPS

Once they're made, wrapped loops can be joined with jump rings or while you're forming one of them. Just before you begin making a wrap, thread it through the completed loop on another component.

DOUBLE-ENDED WRAPPED LOOPS

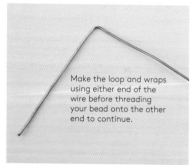

Make the loop and wraps using either end of the wire before threading your bead onto the other end to continue.

For a wrapped loop on either side of a bead, begin with a right-angle bend in the wire, at least 1½ in/4cm from the end. Follow Steps 4–9 on pages 70–71 to make a wrapped loop, add a bead, and make another wrap above it.

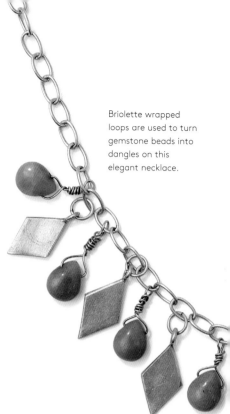

Briolette wrapped loops are used to turn gemstone beads into dangles on this elegant necklace.

DECORATED BEAD

STEP 1
Cut 4½ in/11.5cm of wire and make a bend 1½ in/4cm from the end. Make a wrapped loop with one or two wraps. Trim the wire and thread on a large bead.

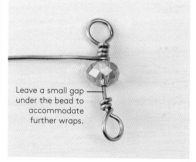

Leave a small gap under the bead to accommodate further wraps.

STEP 2
Make a right-angle bend above the bead slightly farther away than you usually would. Begin your wrapped loop, stopping ⅛ in/3mm away from the bead.

STEP 3
Holding the bead against the wraps you just made, wrap the wire—by hand, if necessary, so that you can get close to the bead—all around the bead and down to the bottom of it.

BRIOLETTE WRAPPED LOOP

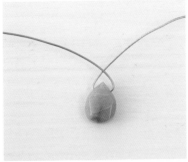

STEP 1

If you want to make just one loop and have it sit centrally above a drop or pendant bead, begin by threading wire through the bead hole. Then bend both ends of the wire so that they cross over the top of the bead.

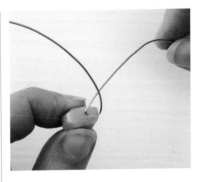

STEP 2

Make sure that the wires cross centrally and that the bead can easily move at all times. Unlike regular beads, drop beads don't have holes through the fatter central section and so are more fragile—if they are held too tightly, they may crack.

The extra wraps fill the gap left previously.

STEP 4

Wrap between the bead and the first wrapped loop to secure the end of the wire and decorative wraps. Trim and neaten as in a normal wrapped loop.

STEP 3

Using flat-nose pliers, bend one end of the wire so that it points straight up and the other so that it sticks out to one side at right angles to the other. As before, make sure that the bead can easily move.

STEP 4

Wrap the wire that's out to the side around the other end as many times as desired and trim. Use the other end to make a simple loop (see pages 68–69). The advantage of this method is that the loop can easily be opened to hang the piece.

Hammering can add more texture and interest to your work. It's also fun to do and great for getting your frustrations out!

Hammering

As beautiful as wire and wirework look, altering that look with hammering can give a whole new visual dimension to your work. In addition to being a decorative technique, hammering also has practical applications—it can be used to work harden your wire and increase its strength. So gather the few tools needed and add this easy-to-use technique to your repertoire.

The wirework hearts sitting at the center of these earrings have been hammered to add texture.

 CLINIC : HAMMERING IS A NOISY AND AGGRESSIVE TECHNIQUE. OVERCOME ANY FEARS WITH THESE SIMPLE STEPS.

- **Being aware of safety issues** should be a top priority when hammering, both for yourself and your wirework.

- **Reducing the noise is easy**— place a folded towel or similar under your hammering block to deaden the noise, keep the block from slipping, and protect your work surface.

- **Begin by experimenting with samples** so that you don't mind how they turn out. Also, remember that this is an organic technique with sometimes unpredictable results, which is all part of the fun.

SAFETY FIRST

Leave a long stem to allow you to hold your work safely.

Always make sure your fingers are as far from the hammer head as possible—leave a "handle" or stem on your work.

HAMMERING WITH BEADS ON

It is always best to hammer your work before you add beads, but if this isn't an option, you can use a wallpaper scraper or similar to guide the hammer to where you want it to go.

FLATTENING YOUR WORK

For a less marked but flattened look, use the flat side of your hammer. Make sure to keep it level and not catch any of the wire with the edges of the hammer.

HARDENING YOUR WORK

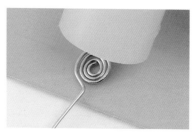

As well as creating a decorative finish, hammering can also be used to work harden your wire or components and add strength. Do this by hammering them flat, using a wooden or plastic hammer and a plastic board to avoid marking the wire.

Capturing the natural beauty of peacock tail feathers, this necklace by Abby Hook was made by applying hammering, layering, weaving, and binding techniques. The pear-shaped central detail is surrounded by swirls of wire, which have been hammered, coiled, wrapped, and woven to create the "feather."

4 ESSENTIAL INGREDIENTS FOR SUCCESSFUL HAMMERING

- **Different hammers** will give you different results (small or large, metal, wood or plastic, smooth or rough), so experiment and see which you prefer.

- **A metal or soft plastic block** can be purchased or you could use something you already have at home. A metal block will help flatten your wirework, while a plastic one will absorb the impact and let your wirework harden with less marking.

- **Samples of wirework coils** are great to have on hand because the thought of damaging your work can be offputting. Begin by making up plenty of samples, then practice the technique and find your personal preferences.

- **An enthusiastic you**—with a willingness to experiment and judge the results—is essential to creating your own look.

ADDING TEXTURE

Adding texture through hammering gives your work dents and marks that catch the light. The rounded end of your hammer is ideal for this. If you want a different look, use the edges of the flat end.

Unhammered, the wire in your coil will still be rounded.

When hammered with the flat side of your hammer, the wire in your coil will flatten out.

When hit with the rounded end of your hammer, the wire will flatten out and have dents in it.

Handmade wire tubes are a funky decorative element that you can use in many different ways.

Making tubes

Taking your wirework to another level by forming wirework tubes gives you a brand-new design component that can be used in a multitude of exciting ways. With a little practice, you can soon be winding out lengths of attractive tubes that will only enhance your jewelry's attractiveness.

This inventive ring combines two silver wire tubes threaded onto extra wire, with a simple loop at either end. There are also simple loops around the feature bead.

MAKING TUBES USING PLIERS

STEP 1
Using your round-nose pliers, make a loop at one end of your wire by turning your pliers away from you. At this point, don't center the loop or make it the size you would like the diameter of your tube to be.

STEP 2
Place your loop on your pliers and slightly rotate the pliers away from you. At the same time, press the wire onto the pliers to form the tube, using your fingers and thumb to make the coils against the pliers.

Keep the coils tight against one other.

STEP 3
Make sure the new coils are forming on the same part of the pliers (you can mark the pliers if this helps) and the old coils come off the end of the pliers. Keep rotating and pressing.

STEP 4
Make the tube as long or as short as you want. Remove from the pliers and trim close to the end of the last coil to neaten.

MAKING TUBES USING THREE-STEP PLIERS

Using three-step pliers will help to keep your tube the same size throughout. Simply decide which step to use and stay on it for the whole length of the coil.

To make this bracelet, two silver wire tubes were threaded onto extra wire and simple loops were added at each end. Then the simple loops were linked with beads joined with wrapped loops.

3 WAYS TO MAKE YOUR TUBES THE SAME SIZE

- **Use three-step wire looping pliers** (which can save you money, since they can also be used to make jump rings). One side is similar to round-nose pliers but with three ridged edges to create three sizes of loops or rings. The other side is concave so that the loops remain round as they are formed.

- **Form your tubes around a dowel, pen tube, or metal rod,** such as those designed and sold for the task. Or use a knitting needle.

- **Mark your pliers** with a permanent marker or tape and stay on the mark.

USING THE TUBES

The tubes can be used as components by themselves by bending out the final coil on each end. These will act as simple loops to join onto other components.

You can also thread your tube onto a length of wire and make a simple loop at either end. This adds strength and allows you to form and bend the piece.

Wirework tubes can also be used as beads. Cut them to different lengths, then string them as decorative elements onto beading wire, elastic, memory wire, or another material.

When threaded onto other wire, tubes can be formed and bent into different shapes, as in these earrings. Here they form a frame to showcase some briolette wrapped loops.

Wire coils can be large or small, hammered or plain, simple or adorned. Whichever you choose, the end result will be both whimsical and delicate.

Making coils

Wirework coils are easy to learn and their unique and organic nature means that no two are exactly alike. A simple wrist rotation is all you need to create these circular shapes. Once they are formed, how you use them and how much you dress them up is entirely up to you.

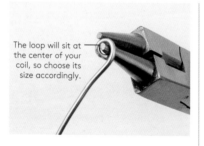

The loop will sit at the center of your coil, so choose its size accordingly.

STEP 1
Carefully cut a 4 in/10cm piece of wire. Using the tip of your round-nose pliers, make a small loop, and stop when the wire touches itself. If you want a different look at the center of your coil, you can make a larger loop.

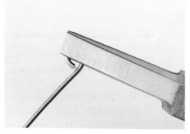

STEP 2
Using your dominant hand, pick up the loop with your flat-nose pliers and hold it securely. The loop should be lying on its side, with the tail of the wire pointing away from you. Having the wire pointing away makes it much easier to form the coil.

Small silver coils with a bead on top and a simple loop dress up these purchased earring findings.

Your thumb helps to form the coil against the wire already coiled.

STEP 3
Gently rotate your dominant hand away from you and use the thumb of your other hand to press the wire onto the loop. You are using the loop as the form to make the coil.

STEP 4
Continue rotating and pressing until the coil is the desired size. Using your flat-nose pliers, make a bend in the wire right next to the coil. Make sure that the wire comes out at a right angle to the coil.

STEP 5
Thread a bead onto the wire (if this is part of your design), then add a simple loop to finish. If you want to hammer the coil, do this before adding the bead and the loop, taking care not to hammer the stem too flat.

CLINIC : HOW TO BECOME A CONFIDENT COIL MAKER

- **Practice makes perfect!** Don't expect every coil to come out right the first time. Use leftover pieces of wire from other projects to hone your technique until you are confident.

- **Not all wire is the same—some are more flexible than others.** Start with inexpensive copper wire, which is relatively soft and easy to work, before experimenting with more expensive wires such as sterling silver or harder wires such as brass or steel.

3 QUICK WAYS TO ALTER A COIL

- **Hammer it** to add texture or flatten it.

- **Make a larger or smaller loop** to sit at the center.

- **Experiment** with making the coils less even.

USING COILS

Coils can be turned into charms and dangles with the simple addition of a simple loop. They can then be threaded onto a stringing material or hung from wirework or the links of a chain.

If you form a large loop above your coil (so that it lies at right angles to the coil), leave a length of straight wire, then file the end, you will have made a unique earring.

Adding a bead above a coil, hammered or not, gives it color and interest. This component can now be strung or dangled from the link of a chain or another piece of wirework.

A bead cage is formed by making two coils on one wire, spiraling in different directions, until they touch. The coil centers are then folded over and teased out to form the shape. The inner loop at each end can be used to string the cage.

Hammered coils dress up the most basic of beads.

Findings are essential to all jewelry making. Being able to design and create your own will save you money and give you more control over your creative vision.

Making your own findings

The world of findings can be a dazzling yet expensive one. But if you examine them closely, you'll soon see that many of them are made using the same wirework techniques as the rest of your jewelry. With this knowledge and some basic instructions, designing your own findings can be a satisfying finish to your original piece.

JUMP RINGS

STEP 1

These essential findings are rings made from individual coils of wirework tubes. Begin by making a tube using pliers, a metal rod, or a wooden dowel (or even a pen) so that the loops are the size you need (see pages 76–77).

Place the flat side of your cutters against the wire that you want to keep.

STEP 2

Carefully trim the end of the tube, using the flat end of your cutters against the wire that you want to keep. This gives a flatter cut, which means that the ends of your rings will fit more closely and neatly together.

STEP 3

Turn your cutters and cut off an entire loop, this time using the flat end of the cutters against the loop you're cutting away so that both ends of the individual ring are flat.

STEP 4

Re-trim the end of the tube with the flat side of the cutters against it. Continue cutting off individual loops, rotating the cutters each time and re-trimming the tube end before making the next jump ring.

Copper S-hook clasps, along with handmade jump rings, are used as both clasps and decorative components in this wrapped bead necklace.

S-HOOK CLASPS

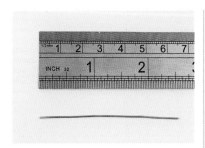

STEP 1

These great clasps are simple to make and can be resized and adjusted as desired. Begin by cutting a 2¹/₂ in/6cm length of 20ga/0.8mm or thicker wire. Straighten the cut wire by running it through your hands.

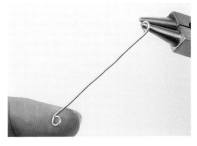

STEP 2

Grasp one end of your wire with the point of your round-nose pliers and form a small, tight loop. Repeat at the other end of your wire, but form second loop on the other side, facing the opposite way.

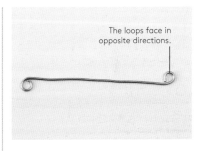

The loops face in opposite directions.

STEP 3

If the second loop isn't facing the right way, simply place either loop flat inside your flat-nose pliers and rotate the loop or the whole wire until the loops are facing in opposite directions.

STEP 4

Using your round-nose pliers, hold just under one of the small loops, making sure that the loop is touching the jaw of the pliers. Pull the wire around the jaw until it touches the small loop.

STEP 5

Make another large loop at the other end of the wire in exactly the same way. Again, you want the two loops to be diagonally opposite each other. If they aren't, adjust them using your hands and pliers.

continued ⟶

EARRING FINDINGS

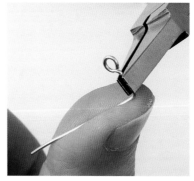

STEP 1
Cut two pieces of 22–24ga/0.6–0.5mm wire 1³/₄ in/4.5cm long. Using your round-nose pliers, make a small centralized simple loop at one end of one of the pieces of wire. Repeat on the other wire.

STEP 2
Using your flat-nose pliers, hold one of the pieces of wire just above the loop and bend it to create a right angle. Repeat on the other piece of wire, matching up the distances between the loops and the bends.

STEP 3
Grasp the bend on one piece of wire with the base of your round-nose pliers. Bend the long length of wire around the pliers to form a loop. Continue bending the wire until it points down toward the original loop. Repeat on the other wire.

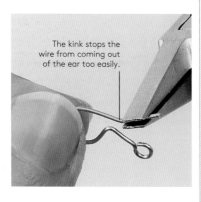

The kink stops the wire from coming out of the ear too easily.

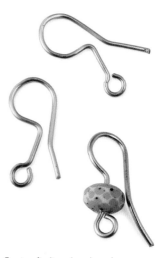

STEP 4
Gently add a kink to the long length of wire. Then trim to the desired length and file carefully to remove any burrs or sharpness. Repeat on the other wire.

STEP 5
If you want a more decorative ear wire, thread a small bead or coil onto the wire between the two loops.

Earring findings hand made from copper wire can be decorated with beads and made to suit your own preferences.

These striking earrings have long handmade earring findings that are adorned with beads, threaded on between the two loops.

EYE PINS AND HEAD PINS

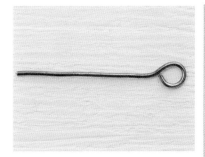

MAKING YOUR OWN
Although you can purchase these, they are very easy to make and you'll always have some on hand in just the size you want. Simply cut a length of wire and, using the appropriate part of your round-nose pliers, form a neat, simple loop.

ADDING A STOPPER
This sits at the end of the wire to stop your bead from falling off. One decorative method is to use a wire coil, which you can make as large or small as you wish.

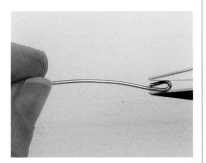

SUBTLE HEAD PIN
To make a subtle head pin, simply grasp the wire end with your flat-nose pliers and bend it to form a "U"-shape. You can then flatten this with flat-nose pliers if you wish.

SPECIAL HEAD PIN
One way to make a special head pin is to hammer the end of your wire so it is flat and wide enough to stop your bead from falling off. Either leave the unique shape you have made or file to adjust and soften it.

4 TOP TIPS FOR GOOD-LOOKING FINDINGS

- **Work on making matching findings, such as ear wires, one step at a time** rather than finishing one and trying to match the other to it afterward—you'll get much better results.

- **Make the size and scale appropriate** for the piece of jewelry you're making.

- **Vary the look of your jewelry** by choosing the color of your wire to coordinate or contrast with the rest of the piece.

- **Take inspiration from purchased findings** to see all the extra details and differences that you can apply to your own pieces.

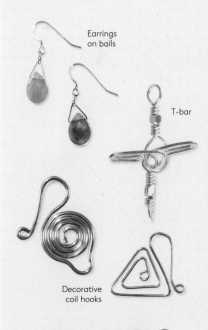

Earrings on bails

T-bar

Decorative coil hooks

Double hook-and-eye fastener

Chains can form the perfect base for much of your jewelry. Knowing how to make your own will save you time and money and allow you to experiment more creatively.

Making your own chains

Purchased chains come in a wide variety of styles and price ranges. Learning how to make your own will not only cost less but will also allow you to be creative and make your mark in jewelry design. However you use the chain, knowing that you made it yourself makes the piece unique and special to you or the recipient.

MAKING A BASIC LINKED CHAIN

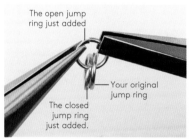

Large jump rings are simply linked together for sections of chain in this silver and amethyst necklace/belt.

STEP 1
This type of chain is made by joining jump rings together until you have the desired length. To save time when actually linking the rings, begin by opening lots of jump rings and closing other rings securely.

STEP 2
Link an open jump ring through a closed one. Thread another closed ring onto the open one. Now close the open ring and you'll have joined three rings together, even though you had to close only one.

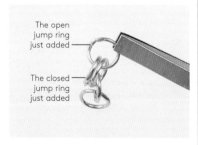

STEP 3
Using an open ring, pick up another closed ring. Thread the open ring through a ring at the end of the chain you have started. Close the new open ring and you'll have added on two rings.

STEP 4
Continue using open rings to link closed rings to the end of your chain, making sure you close the new ring securely each time. Repeat until the chain is as long as desired.

MULTI-LINK CHAINS

These are a more decorative version of the basic linked chain. They are made by picking up three or more closed jump rings each time and then either leaving just one single ring in between or filling in the single ring space with more open rings.

A handmade twisted link chain forms the base for this charm bracelet.

MAKING A TWISTED LINK CHAIN

STEP 1
This chain is a more ornate version of a basic linked chain, but it is built in a similar way. Begin by joining two jump rings together, then holding them so that they overlap each other.

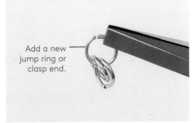

Add a new jump ring or clasp end.

STEP 2
You may find it easier to hold both rings if you attach another jump ring to them (see above) or even one end of a clasp. This gives you something extra to hold onto and stops the rings from moving around.

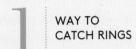

1 | WAY TO CATCH RINGS

If you are sitting down, use a flat dish towel or similar as your work surface, tucking it into your collar so that any dropped rings don't fall to the floor but instead land on your chest within easy reach of your pliers. You can also wear an apron and spread it onto your work surface so that it performs the same role.

The new open jump ring

The extra jump ring, to help you hold your work

STEP 3
Attach another open jump ring to the two overlapped rings, making sure that you pass it through both of them and they are still overlapping. Close the new ring securely and neatly.

New jump ring

The two overlapped rings from Step 1

The extra jump ring, to help you hold your work

STEP 4
Take another open jump ring and attach it to the two rings from Step 1, making sure you pass it through both of them. Before closing the ring, loop it through the last new ring that was added so that they are twisted together. Close the ring.

STEP 5
Repeat Steps 3–4, adding pairs of rings so that the first is attached to the previous pair. The second one should also be attached to the same pair and should link through the first ring of the new pair. Always make sure that each new ring is securely and neatly closed.

Quick
start
project:

Turquoise and copper coils necklace

Test your new-found wirework skills and get coiling for this fast and fabulous necklace project that combines turquoise beads and copper wire.

MATERIALS AND TOOLS

- 80 in (200cm) of 20ga/0.8mm wire
- 2¹/₂ in (6cm) of 18ga/1mm wire (or 20ga/0.8mm if that's what you have) or a purchased S-hook clasp
- 25 x 6mm turquoise beads
- Round-nose pliers
- Flat-nose pliers
- Wire cutters
- Hammer and hammering surface (optional)

TECHNIQUES See also:

- Working with wire, pages 64–65
- Hammering, pages 74–75
- Making coils, pages 78–79

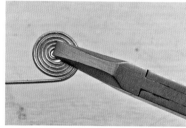

STEP 1
Carefully cut a 6 in (15cm) length of 20ga/0.8mm wire and add a simple loop at the end. Using your flat-nose pliers, begin making a coil and stop when you have ¹/₂ in (1cm) of wire left. Repeat to make seven more coils.

STEP 2
This step is optional but adds texture and interest to your piece. Place a coil on a hard surface and hammer as desired. Repeat for all of the coils or as many as you wish, taking care not to hammer the "stem" on each.

STEP 3
Using your hands and working close, bend the stem on one of your coils so that it sits at right angles to the coil. Using your round-nose pliers, make a simple loop, trimming your wire as required. Repeat on all the coils.

STEP 4
Now you need to adjust the coils so that they lie flat when you wear the necklace. Grasp a loop in your flat-nose pliers and hold the coil firmly in your hand or in flat-nose pliers. Rotate the loop so that it lies perpendicular to your coil. Repeat on all the coils.

STEP 5
Thread a bead onto the long length of wire, make a simple loop at the end. Slide the bead to the loop, cut the wire, then make another loop. Repeat for all beads, making a single larger loop on two components (to attach your clasp).

STEP 6
If you are making your own S-hook clasp, take the 2½ in/6cm length of 18ga/1mm wire (or cut 2½ in/6cm of 20ga/0.8mm wire) and make a simple loop at each end. Rotate the loops to face in opposite directions.

STEP 7
Using the base of your round-nose pliers, make a large loop at either end of your clasp and adjust as needed to form a perfect S-hook. If wished, hammer for strength and decorative effect.

STEP 8
To help plan your final design, lay all the pieces on a flat surface or bead design board, and adjust as desired. If you find that you need more components, then make them to match those you already have.

STEP 9
Carefully join the simple loop components to match your planned design, making sure you add the components with the larger loops at each end of the piece.

3 TYPES OF WIRE YOU MIGHT USE FOR THIS PROJECT

- 20ga/0.8mm is perfect for making the coils and bead component.

- 18ga/1mm will give your clasp added strength.

- 22ga/0.6mm might be necessary if the holes in your beads are too small to fit anything larger.

3 SIMPLE VARIATIONS YOU CAN DO

- Skip the beads altogether and use handmade wire tubes for decoration instead.

- If you don't have quite enough beads, join your components using jump rings to make them spread further.

- Vary the size of your coils and then arrange them from largest to smallest, from the center outward, for a graduated look.

3 GREAT COLOR COMBINATIONS YOU CAN USE WITH COPPER

- Turquoise and all blues are a natural contrast to copper.

- Reds and oranges make for a harmonious and matching color scheme.

- Greens go perfectly with copper, especially if you allow the copper to tarnish!

Guest Designer KRISTIN SMITH

❝ I am the owner of K S Jewellery Designs, and I design and make silver and gemstone wirework and metalwork jewelry. I have written many wirework tutorials and my designs are influenced by the simple lines and shapes found in nature. You can see my work at www.ksjewellerydesigns.co.uk. ❞

Ornate frame earrings

Use wirework and hammering techniques to create eye-catching circular frame earrings, adding spirals and sparkling briolettes for a touch of elegance.

MATERIALS AND TOOLS

- 20½ in (52cm) of 20ga (0.8mm) soft round wire
- 31½ in (80cm) of 26ga (0.4mm) soft round wire
- 2 briolette beads (approximately 8mm x 8mm)
- Ruler or measuring tape
- Round dowel or thick pen, ½ in (1.2cm) in diameter
- Chain-nose pliers
- Wire cutters
- Round-nose pliers
- Nylon-headed pliers
- Chasing hammer
- Stainless-steel bench block
- Emery paper: medium, fine, very fine
- Silver polishing cloth
- Pencil, paper, and ruler

TECHNIQUES See also:

Measuring, cutting, and filing, page 62
Wrapped loops, page 70
Hammering, page 74
Making coils, page 78
Earring findings, page 82

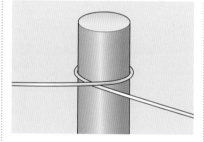

STEP 1
Run 16 in (40cm) of 20ga (0.8mm) soft round wire between nylon-headed pliers to straighten it. Leave about 1 in (2.5cm) from the cut end of the wire and wrap the wire around the dowel or pen to make a circle.

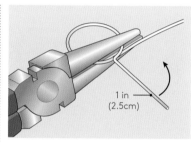

STEP 2
Gently grip the circle with a pair of chain-nose pliers just above where the wires cross. With your fingers, make a slight bend in the short length of wire. Then make two wraps around it with the rest of the wire.

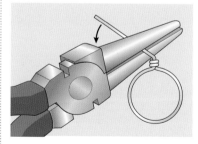

STEP 3
Cut the wire behind the two wraps with wire cutters. Squeeze the cut end between your chain-nose pliers and sand down any rough bits with emery paper. Bend the short wire to one side.

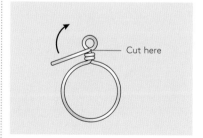

STEP 4
Make a little loop in the short wire by shaping the wire around round-nose pliers. Cut off the excess wire. Use chain-nose pliers to flatten and squeeze the little loop closed.

BEADER'S WISDOM

● ● ●

Plated wire is not recommended for the hammering and sanding elements of this project, because it can become brittle and the surface covering might be damaged. I use sterling-silver or fine silver wire for my final jewelry pieces, but I do recommend practicing designs first with less expensive wire, such as soft copper wire.

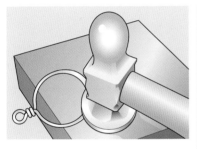

STEP 5
Place the circle to the edge of the stainless-steel block and gently hammer all around the circle to spread out the wire and fix the shape. Turn the wire piece around and gently hammer the little loop as well.

STEP 6
Repeat Steps 1 to 5 to create a second circular-frame wire piece. Lay them together to ensure they are the same size. If they are not the same size, re-make one.

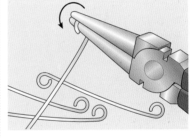

STEP 7
Cut four x 1³/₄ in (4.5cm) lengths of 20ga (0.8mm) wire and sand the ends with emery paper. Create little loops at the end of each wire piece with round-nose pliers, making sure that the loops curl in the opposite direction to each other.

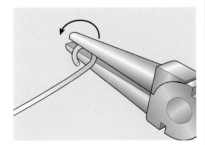

STEP 8
Grip one of the loops between your chain-nose pliers. Hold the rest of the wire with your other hand. Carefully turn the pliers to bend the wire around the little loop, leaving a gap around the loop. Release the pliers.

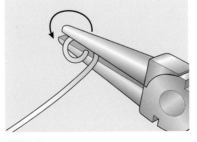

STEP 9
Grip the little loop again along with some of the curved wire. Turn the pliers again to continue the curve. Try to keep the gap between the loop and the curved wire even.

STEP 10
Repeat Step 9 until you have created a little open spiral at the end of the wire. Turn the wire piece around and create a similar open spiral at the other end.

Kristin Smith

4 WAYS TO MINIMIZE TOOL MARKS WHEN USING PLIERS

- Use your fingers as much as possible to manipulate the wire.
- Use nylon-headed pliers where possible.
- Buy the best-quality metal pliers you can afford that have smooth jaws.
- When using pliers, only grip the wire as firmly as you need to without over-squeezing.

3 WAYS TO MINIMIZE TOOL MARKS WHEN USING A HAMMER

- Make sure your hammer head and bench block have a clean and smooth surface.
- Try to hammer straight down rather than at an angle.
- Using a hammer with rounded edges will help to minimize hammer marks.

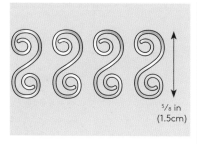

STEP 11
Repeat Steps 8 to 10 to create open spirals on the other three wire pieces. Each spiral wire piece should be about ⁵/₈ in (1.5cm) long.

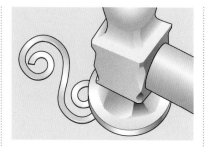

STEP 12
Gently hammer the four spiral wire pieces to spread the wire and fix the shape.

STEP 13
Lay out your wire pieces to check that the two earrings will look similar. Adjust the spirals if necessary. To give the wire pieces a shiny finish, rub them all over with very fine emery paper and then rub them with a silver polishing cloth.

STEP 14
Cut off a 12 in (30cm) length of 26ga (0.4mm) round soft wire. Bend the wire in the middle and insert it into the bottom of one of the circles. Make four tight wraps with the wire. Push the wraps together with your fingernails.

STEP 15
Place one of the wire spirals behind the lower edge of one circle. Wrap up the side of the circle, making sure that you also wrap around the spiral at the two points where it touches the circle.

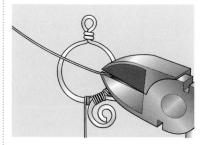

STEP 16
Keep wrapping until the spiral is secure. Make sure that your wraps are neat and even, using your fingernails to push them together or spread them out. Snip the wire off behind the circle and push the cut wire down with chain-nose pliers.

FINISHED SIZE
Approximately 1 in (2.5cm)
wide x 2 in (5cm) long,
including earwires.

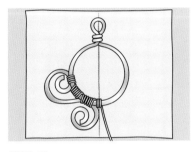

STEP 17

Draw a line on a piece of paper and
lay the piece down along it to help you
check the symmetry of the earring and
the placement of the spiral. Repeat
Steps 15 and 16 to attach a second
spiral to the other side of the circle.

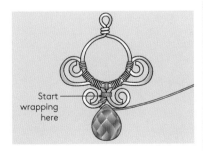

Start
wrapping
here

STEP 18

Cut a 4 in (10cm) length of 26ga
(0.4mm) wire. Make four wraps where
the two spiral pieces meet and four
wraps down one spiral. Slide a briolette
bead along the wire and push it into
place. Next make four wraps up the
other spiral.

STEP 19

Snip off the excess wire at the back
and push down the cut wires. Repeat
Steps 14 to 18 to make the second
earring. Attach simple ear wires made
from 1¹/₂ in/4cm of 20ga/0.8mm soft
round wire (see page 82) through the
little loops at the top of the earrings.

Guest Designer ABBY HOOK

" I am the author of *Wire Jewelry Masterclass* and specialize in cold connection wire jewelry making. I have loved making wire jewelry since childhood and I enjoy sharing my passion with others. You can see my work at www.abbyhook.co.uk. "

Mermaid's teardrop necklace

Use woven wire to secure and embellish a stone drop, with Celtic-inspired hammered wire, to create this clean, flowing design.

MATERIALS AND TOOLS

- 17 in (43cm) of 12ga/2mm soft round wire
- 70 in (178cm) of 21ga/0.7mm soft round wire
- 60 in (152cm) of 24ga/0.5mm soft round wire
- 1 x drop-shaped focal stone (front drilled), 1 1/2 in (4cm) high x 1 in (3cm) wide
- 7 x 6mm round beads (6 on chain, 1 on focal stone)
- 1 x 4mm round bead
- 4 x 15mm oval beads
- 2 x 25mm oblong beads
- Wire cutters suitable for 12ga/2mm wire
- Tape measure
- Marker pen
- Round-nose pliers
- Ring mandrel
- Bench block or anvil
- Chasing hammer
- File
- Sanding pads, 3 grits: 180, 220, and 280
- Nylon-jaw pliers
- Chain-nose pliers
- Flat-nose pliers
- Flush-cutters

TECHNIQUES See also:

Measuring, cutting, filing, page 62
Wrapped loops, page 70
Hammering, page 74

STEP 1
Cut a piece of 12ga/2mm wire 14 in (35.5cm) long. Mark the centerpoint with a marker pen to help you keep the design symmetrical. Using the round-nose pliers, form a large round loop in each end of the wire.

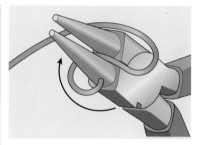

STEP 2
Grasp the wire just after the loop with the thickest point of the round-nose pliers. Pull the wire around the pliers with your non-dominant hand to form a shepherd's hook. Repeat on the other end. The wire will now be 9 1/2 in (24cm) long.

STEP 3
Using the penmark as guidance, shape the wire around the thickest point of your ring mandrel so that it crosses at the top, creating a drop shape. Check that the frame is symmetrical and that the stone fits inside.

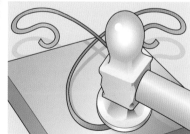

STEP 4
The frame should now measure 4 1/3 in (11cm) wide x 2 3/4 in (7cm) high. Place the wire in the center of the bench block or anvil and carefully hammer the curve of the drop and each end of the frame.

BEADER'S WISDOM
• ● ●

To make sure that a loop is round, first shape the wire around the round-nose pliers. Notice how the first part of the wire is straight, despite shaping it around a curved item. Hold the wire cutters at a 90° angle to the straight part of the wire and snip the end off. This angled end will now close snugly against the straight wire, giving you a perfectly round loop.

FINISHED SIZE
Chain length 16 in (40.5cm); pendant 2$\frac{1}{4}$ x 1$\frac{3}{8}$ in (5.7 x 3.5cm)

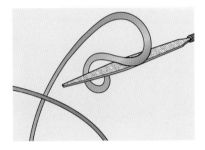

STEP 5
File the ends of the wire to form a smooth curve and remove any imperfections on the frame. Sand the ends with the sanding pads, using each one in an opposite direction to the last, until you have achieved a high shine.

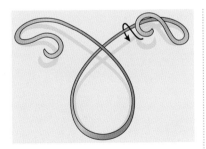

STEP 6
Check that the frame is symmetrical and that the stone fits with enough clearance to allow the weaving wire to pass through. Push one loop upward so that it crosses over the top of the frame and the open loop hooks behind. Squeeze together with nylon-jaw pliers. Repeat with the other loop.

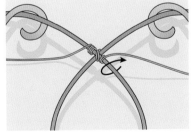

STEP 7
Cut 60 in (152cm) of 24ga/0.5mm wire. Measure a 10 in (25cm) tail and attach it to the frame on the straight wire, coiling it three times. Keep the wire at 90° to the frame so that the coils are straight. Bind the crossover twice to secure the frame together and coil the loop twice.

STEP 8
Bring the weaving wire under the right wire of the frame and over the left, pulling it tightly. Using the end of the wire as a needle, pull the length through, pushing your finger into the loop created to stop it from twisting and creating kinks.

Abby Hook

4 TIPS FOR SUCCESSFUL HAMMERING

- Keep the hammer head at 90° to the bench block to be sure of a flat, even finish.
- Always hammer in the center of the bench block to avoid creating indents.
- Keep checking that the stone fits in the frame—hammering can distort the shape.
- Notice the frame curving upward as you hammer.

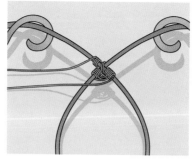

STEP 9

Coil the weaving wire once around the left wire of the frame to secure it in place. Take the weaving wire under the left frame wire and over the right, and coil it once. Continue until there are seven complete weaves. Keep sliding the weave up the frame to keep it tight.

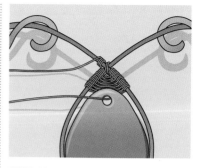

STEP 10

Hold the stone in position. Thread the wire behind the frame and the stone, through the hole to the front, and around the left side of the frame. Coil the wire once to secure. Repeat on the right side of the frame, again coiling the wire once.

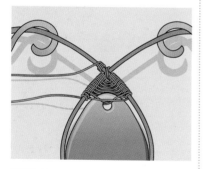

STEP 11

The weave must be well formed to hold the stone firmly in place. Pass the weaving wire under the right frame wire, up between frame and stone, over the stone, and down between the stone and left frame wire. Coil it once around the left frame wire to secure.

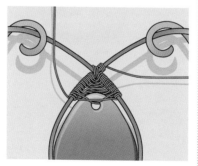

STEP 12

Turn the frame over, so that you working on the back, and take the weaving wire over the left frame wire, behind the stone, and over the right frame wire. Coil once to secure. Make sure that the weave wires are straight, and use the tension on the coil to secure the weave in place. The picture shows the back view.

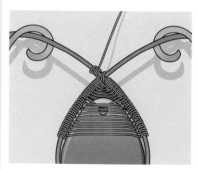

STEP 13

Weave ten times over the front of the stone and coil the frame wire three times to secure. Trim the wire on the inside of the frame and tuck it in by using a crimping motion with the chain-nose pliers, pushing the end tight against the frame.

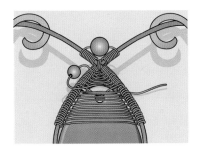

STEP 14
Coil the left arm of the frame ten times with the 10 in (25cm) tail. Add a 6mm bead and secure it to the right arm, coiling it ten times. Pass the wire to the front, add a 4mm bead, and secure it to the back of the weave by coiling it three times. Trim and tuck in.

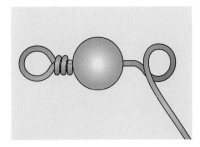

STEP 15
Cut a 3 in (7.5cm) length of 21ga/0.7mm wire. Measure 1¼ in (3cm) and make a 45° bend, shape around the round-nose pliers, and then wrap the wire around itself three times. Trim and tuck the end in. Thread a 6mm bead onto the wire. Repeat on the other end.

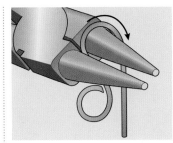

STEP 16
For each of the 25mm oblongs and the 15mm ovals, cut a 10 in (25cm) piece of 21ga/0.7mm wire and form a wrapped link in the center, leaving a 3–3½ in (7.5–9cm) tail wire. Bring the tail wire around over the stone and coil it over the existing coils.

STEP 17
To make the clasp, cut a piece of 12ga/2mm wire 3 in (7.5cm) long. Make a round loop in one end. Grasp the wire just above the loop with the round-nose pliers and shape the wire around the thickest part of the jaw, creating a hook shape.

STEP 18
Hammer the loop and hook of the clasp to flatten and harden the wire. Hold the clasp at 90° to the bench block so that it points straight up and hammer the end so that it bends up very slightly. File and sand to finish.

STEP 19
Referring to the photo at right, connect all the components together, remembering to thread the previous link onto the new one before closing. (Each side of the chain should look the same.) Remember to make the loops slightly larger to attach to the frame.

CHAPTER 4

Beadwork

With only a needle, thread, and the tiniest of glass beads, you can stitch together a stunning creation. This chapter will teach you the most useful beadweaving stitches and show you how to combine seed beads with larger beads and components. Add bead looming and crystal bezeling to your beading skills for beautiful finishing touches.

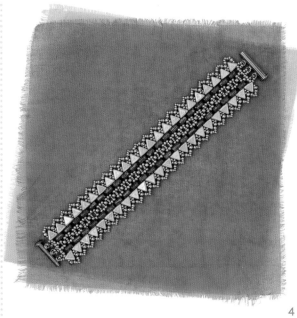

Beadwork:
be inspired

1. SIAN NOLAN Sian's pendants use a mix of seed beads, pearls, and crystals combined with cubic right-angle weave (see page 134) to create eye-catching and interchangeable pieces.

2. MARIE NEW Marie's wondrously sparkling pendant involves a 27mm crystal bezeled using a mix of different beads. Mixing peyote stitches and RAW (see pages 124 and 128) allows the designer to encase the crystal to perfection.

3. SIAN NOLAN A complete mix of beads and techniques unite in Sian's beautiful slider beads that allow the wearer to mix-and-match as desired.

4. NORMA JEAN DELL This bracelet uses a clever modification of right-angle weave (see page 128) to combine two-holed Kheops triangles and Rulla rectangles with seed beads into a timelessly stylish design.

5. SHONA BEVAN In this striking necklace that uses tile beads, crystals, and seeds, Shona has used her extensive knowledge of individual beading stitches and combined

5

6

7

8

them, describing it as "a modified version of right-angle weave."

6. LYNN DAVY Turquoise, tactile, and tempting sums up this necklace! Lynn used a mix of seed beads and gemstone chips in a united color scheme to create this visually flowing piece. But, never one to be boring, she snuck in some red beads to allow the colors to pop. Breaking up a monochrome color scheme in this

way is a surefire way of adding interest and drama.

7. JENNIFER AIRS A monochrome color scheme is anything but boring and plain in this piece, which uses cellini spiral (see page 126) to add drama and visual interest. The use of subtle colors lets the featured lampwork bead take center-stage and be the star of the show, while the movement from lampwork bead

to plain beaded rope through the spiral means that the change in size happens gradually.

8. NORMA JEAN DELL A flexible base of Zulu stitch and structural netting is embellished with brilliant crystal bicones and finished with a sliding clasp.

9

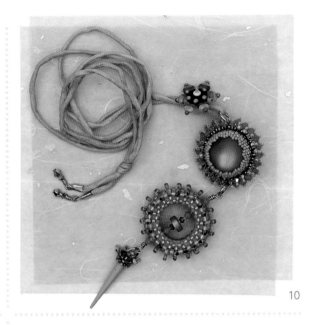

10

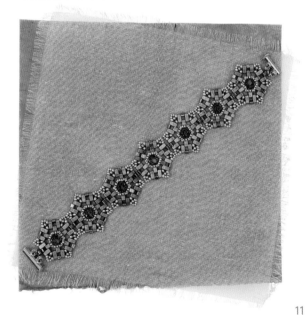

11

12

9. JENNIFER AIRS This striking tubular peyote (see page 124) bracelet combines artisan glass beads with seed beads, fringe drops, and cylinder beads. The beaded clasp is embellished with crystal bicones for added sparkle.

10. SIAN NOLAN Spikes, sparkles, silver, seed beads, and silk combine in this mixed-media necklace. Sian has used a mix of beaded

components that follow a color theme and joined them using wirework.

11. NORMA JEAN DELL Sparkling crystal rounds are enclosed at the centers of linked hexagons made with a peyote-based stitch. Two-holed half-Tila beads mesh seamlessly with seed beads to give lots of geometric detail.

12. LYNN DAVY Beading over a wooden bead has allowed Lynn to create a larger focal point using small beads. Mixed with a simple strung bead necklace and wirework-added charms, this necklace allows the intricate beaded pattern to shine through and not be overwhelmed by its accompaniments.

13

14

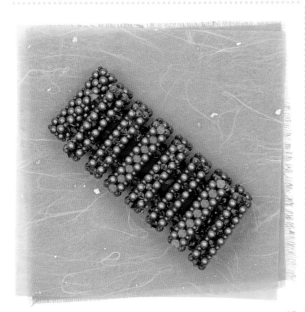

15

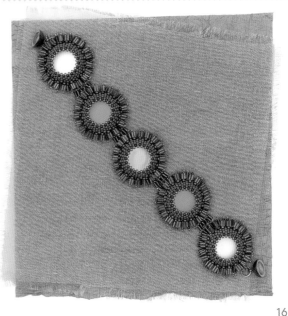

16

13. NORMA JEAN DELL A stunning crystal pendant on a matching beaded necklace. Norma Jean's design combines peyote stitch (see page 124), right-angle weave (see page 128), and cubic right-angle weave (see page 134). Metallic seed beads bring together pearls, glass spikes, and crystals for dramatic, eye-catching impact.

14. JANE LOCK A bangle made of seamless links of peyote stitch (see page 124) in contrasting shades and finishes, Jane's design is an excellent example of how a striking piece can be made with a single stitch and a simple color scheme.

15. SIAN NOLAN An opulent cuff sparkling with crystal bicones, stitched in cubic right-angle weave (see page 134). The crystal colors are

cleverly varied to give the piece subtlety and richness.

16. JANE LOCK Glowing acrylic cabochons are bezeled with seed beads (see page 140) and edged and linked with bugle beads. A magnetic clasp provides a secure fastening without distracting from the colorful beadwork.

Beading is the principle of joining together beads with thread and using different stitches. All of the materials and tools seen below will help to make beading a process you will enjoy.

Essential beadwork tools and supplies

1 NEEDLES
Available in different thicknesses and lengths, beading needles tend to be smaller than sewing needles so you can thread through the small beads multiple times. If you struggle with threading your needles, "Big Eye" versions are available. This is where the eye takes up almost the full length of the needle and can be flexed to open wider for threading.

2 SCISSORS, CUTTERS, AND THREAD ZAPS
Any scissors or cutters will do for thread cutting, but a small, sharp pair will get you closer to your work. You can even buy a thread cutter that can be worn as a pendant but has the blades hidden for safety. A thread zap is a battery-operated tool with a wire end that heats up. This can be used to cut your thread and burn away any frizzy thread ends that you see poking out of your work.

3 BEAD MAT
When beading, you need to use a surface that will stop your beads from rolling around, but one that doesn't have a textured or looped surface (such as a towel), which your needle may get caught in. Bead mats are designed especially for the job and will make your beading life a lot easier. You can buy them in different colors to help you see your beads.

4 THREAD
There are so many different threads available, from cotton or nylon sewing or upholstery threads, through monofilaments originally designed for fishing line, to new threads designed especially for beaders; you'll find every beader has a personal preference and that can change depending on the project. It's best to experiment and find out which one suits you and your beadwork best. Beware when using transparent beads, as your thread will affect the finished look of the beads; however, this can be a design feature.

5 WAX OR CONDITIONER
These are optional extras, but many beaders swear by them to get the tension they desire in their work. Generally, wax will stick your threads together and help you get a tighter tension, while conditioner coats the threads, making them slide against each other and resulting in a looser tension.

6 BEAD SCOOPS
Essential for helping you round up your beads and corral them back into their tubes and bags, bead scoops come in a variety of sizes and shapes, and will become indispensable to you.

7 BEAD LOOM
If you plan on doing any bead loom work, then this is a must-have tool. Available in many different sizes, the size you choose can dictate the size of your finished result.

8 FORMS ON WHICH TO BEAD
You may find that having a form to put your beadwork on, such as a pen or dowel, helps you when you are beading a tubular stitch.

THE BEADS

9 SEED BEADS
These small glass beads are shaped like little ring donuts. Sold in many different sizes (even as little as size 22 and smaller), the most common sizes are 15, 11, 8, and 6. The numbering of the beads is based on approximately how many can fit in 1 in (2.5cm) if laid hole upward. You'll find, though, that the sizing can vary wildly between different manufacturers, and even between different colors from the same maker. Seed beads also come in many different finishes, from opaque matte through color-lined and metallic gloss to everything in between. Each finish will add a different look to your beadwork.

8 | MOST COMMON SEED BEADS AND HOW MANY ARE IN A GRAM

Bead	Number per gram
Size 15 seed beads	250
Size 15 cylinder beads	350
Size 11 seed beads	120
Size 11 cylinder beads	200
Size 10 cylinder beads	108
Size 8 seed beads	36
Size 8 cylinder beads	30
Size 6	18

10 CYLINDER BEADS

A subset of seed beads, cylinder beads are generally sold by their brand name, such as Delicas or Aikos. With their accurate sizing and exacting flat sides (imagine a small section cut from a glass tube), they are perfect for precise and geometric work. They have larger holes than regular seed beads and come in a variety of sizes.

11 SHAPED BEADS

In recent years, the basic shapes such a bugle (long tubes), drops, daggers, cubes, triangles, and rounds have been joined by a whole host of new shapes, such as Duos, Super Duos, O-beads, Tri-beads, pyramids, spikes, Dragon Scales, and many, many more.

12 CRYSTALS

Whether they be inexpensive Chinese or Czech or precision-engineered Austrian, crystals always add a touch of sparkle to beadwork. They are available in thousands of shapes, cuts, colors, and finishes, and you'll soon find lots of excuses to use them in your jewelry. They can be stitched into your work, such as the most common bicone and round beads, or bezeled and adorned, such as rivolis and flat-backs. Either way, crystals will add an extra dimension to your finished pieces.

There are some simple tips and tricks you can learn that will enhance your beadwork and make it a much easier creative process for you.

Basic beading tips

Beginning beadweaving can be a frustrating business. You may find that your beadwork does not look exactly like the pictures in the book on the first attempt, but don't be put off. Try to concentrate on understanding the thread path through the beads and how they connect together. With practice, you will become more confident and your hands will learn how to hold the beads with the correct tension in the thread to make neat, even stitches. If you're learning a new stitch, try using a larger-sized bead than the project suggests—this will make it easier for you to follow where the thread should go and will mean that your work grows more quickly, too.

KNOW THE TERMINOLOGY

"ROW VS ROUND"
"Row" refers to flat beadwork, whereas "round" refers to tubular beadwork.

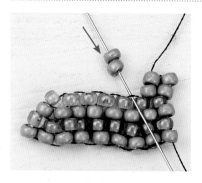

"2-DROP" (OR MORE)
This phrase refers to beading where two or more beads are picked up when beading a stitch, but are treated as a single bead—unlike picking up two beads to increase.

"STEP UP"
This is the maneuver at the end of a round of beadwork, or individual stitches in the case of RAW, where you reposition yourself by threading through one or more beads to be ready to continue the next stitch or round.

WORKING THE BEADS

STOP BEAD
A stop bead prevents the beads from falling off the end of your thread and helps you control your tension. To add one, pick up a seed bead (a different color than you plan to use in your work is best), and circle through it (see below) two or three times, making sure not to pierce the thread so it can be easily removed later.

THREAD THROUGH
Thread through a bead, or beads, in the direction you are already traveling.

CIRCLE THROUGH
Thread through your bead, or beads, in the same direction that you did previously.

THREAD BACK THROUGH
Thread back through your bead, or beads, in the opposite direction to that you did previously.

CLINIC : OVERCOMING CHALLENGES

- **Stuck needle?**
  Never try and pull a needle through with your teeth. Instead, use pliers or a small piece of rubber (from a dishwashing glove, a balloon, or a jar opener, for example) to grip it and pull it through.

- **Correcting a mistake**
  If you ever need to undo your work to correct a mistake, never do it by working backward with your needle on your thread—you'll get into a tangle and pierce your thread. Remove your needle and, gently and slowly, undo the thread, removing beads as far back as needed.

3 GOLDEN RULES FOR WORKING WITH THREAD

- **Adding new threads and finishing old ones.** There are many ways of adding and finishing threads, and you may find your own over time, but the basic principles are about neatly and securely fastening the threads. The simplest, most common method is to weave in new threads and weave out old ones. Weave them through your work, creating thread paths that cross each other for extra security, then trim neatly as needed. It is best to weave in a new thread before weaving away your old one, as it helps you to see where you are in your work.

- **Use a workable length.** Don't use a longer piece of thread than you can easily pull through in one movement. This prevents your thread from getting tangled, speeds up your beading, helps to control your tension, and reduces wear and tear.

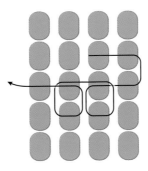

- **Stretching thread.** You will find that if you stretch your beading thread before you use it, it will help to stop tangles as you work. It will also prevent your beadwork from sagging later. Simply pull a length of thread through your hands until it is straight.

4 TIPS TO HELP YOU GET THE BEST OUT OF YOUR BEADS

- **Be careful when buying.** More expensive beads are usually better quality, because of the precision with which they're made as well as the removal of lower-grade beads through quality control. Do your research and look for known brands.

- **Cull your beads.** While misshapen beads can create some unique beadwork, be sure to reject such beads if you want a neat and accurate look to your finished piece.

- **Be aware of bead finishes.** It could be that the finish you have fallen in love with will have worn off before you're even finished beading. While some beads look beautiful as their color fades, others will be a disappointment. Shop carefully and ask your bead supplier for information on the quality of bead finishes.

- **Be strategic with your expensive beads.** 24k gold-plated beads are considerably more expensive than plain glass beads, and it's a waste of money if they are then hidden away within your designs. So, if you plan to embellish you work, or have a back to it that won't be seen, consider using cheaper beads in those spots, saving the best for the front and center.

Multifunctional ladder stitch is not just a stitch in its own right, but is often the beginner's first step into the new world of beadwork.

Ladder stitch

Ladder stitch may seem like a basic technique, but it's essential to know it if you want to go on to brick and herringbone stitch. It will also teach you many of the fundamentals of beading. Here you'll discover how to add beads to create a simple pattern and how to move up to the next level of beading—and before you know it, you'll be creating your own ladder strips.

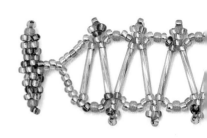

BASIC LADDER STITCH

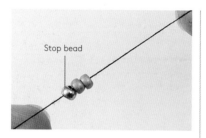

Stop bead

STEP 1
Begin by adding a stop bead to a length of thread, then pick up two new beads. These are the first two beads of your ladder-stitch strip and will soon be sitting side by side, rather than one on top of the other, as they are now.

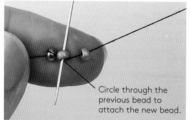

Circle through the previous bead to attach the new bead.

STEP 2
Take your needle and thread and circle through the first bead you picked up. This means you will be threading through it in the same direction your thread has already passed. The second bead will now be joined to the first.

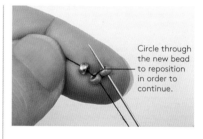

Circle through the new bead to reposition in order to continue.

STEP 3
Take your needle and thread and circle through the second bead you picked up. You will be threading through it in the same direction your thread has already passed.

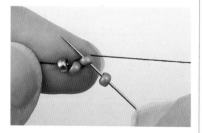

STEP 4
Pick up one new bead and slide it down to meet the others already on your thread. Circle through the bead that it sits next to the second bead, so that the new bead is joined to it.

STEP 5
Circle through the last bead you added, and out. Continue circling and you'll find that you switch from going clockwise to counterclockwise.

STEP 6
Continue adding new beads by picking up a bead, circling through the previous bead (to secure the new one), and then circling through the new bead (to get into position to continue).

This bracelet uses bugle beads laddered together but with extra beads picked up in-between. The full instructions are given below.

3 DIFFERENT LADDER-STITCH LOOKS

- **Make "stacks" or "rungs" in your ladder.** This is called 2-drop (or more) ladder stitch and uses multiple beads instead of single ones. You can also switch from 1- to 2-drop along the length of your work for a wavy look, or graduate between short and tall stacks along the length of your work.

- **Add height with bugle beads.** These long, tube beads sometimes have sharp ends, so adding seed beads at either end will protect your thread.

- **Pick up multiple beads as you work.** If you do this, circle back through some of them only if you want a different look. The bracelet pictured above, at the top of the page, was made so that one seed, one bugle, and one seed are the beads in the stacks (or rungs), but you pick up one seed, one bugle, and six seeds as you go. Only thread back through one seed, the bugle, and one seed to be ready to continue. This leaves five extra seed beads sitting between the stacks. Afterward you can thread back, as was done here, and add little fringes to adorn the bracelet.

JOINING THE ENDS

STEP 7
If you find that the beads aren't sitting nicely next to each other, you can pull the thread to tighten it. You can also use your fingernails to adjust how the beads lie.

Make sure the strip isn't twisted before joining the ends.

STEP 1
When your ladder stitch strip is as long as desired, join the ends to make a continuous piece. Bring both ends of your work together and line them up closely.

THREADING CROSS SECTION | **FIRST LADDER STITCH**

Pick up two beads. Circle through the first to join them, then the second to continue.

THREADING CROSS SECTION | **SUBSEQUENT LADDER STITCHES**

Pick up one new bead. Circle through the previous bead to join them and then the new bead to continue.

STEP 2
Pass the needle out through the last bead added. Continue your circling pattern, circling through the first bead added at the other end of the strip, then back into the last bead to join them together.

Named for its resemblance to brickwork, brick stitch is quick to learn and builds on a ladder-stitch base for a decorative look.

Brick stitch

Easier to learn than many other stitches, brick is a versatile stitch to have in your beading repertoire. It can be used flat or tubular. Once you discover its potential, you can brick stitch to your heart's content, increasing or decreasing as needed. Begin with a ladder-stitch base (see page 106) and add beads to create a piece that evokes the tight, intricate pattern of brickwork.

STARTING AND ENDING A ROW OF BRICK STITCH

Brick-stitch rows may be started and finished in two different ways, based on whether or not the first beads sits "in" or "out." Whichever method you choose, you will need to end the row the opposite way to how you started it in order to keep your beadwork the same width. For example, if you start with an out bead, finish with an in bead. Always starting and ending with out beads is also a great way to increase your work.

It's easy to shape brick stitch into diamonds by increasing and decreasing. These mini-kite earrings by Malobi are made from cylinder beads, which fit neatly together because of their straight sides. A simple pattern emphasizes the geometric shape.

OUT-BEAD START

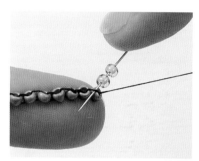

STEP 1
As you bring the needle out of the end bead of your ladder-stitch base, pick up two beads. Thread under the loop of thread that separates the first and second beads in the base.

STEP 2
Thread back through the second bead you picked up, going in the opposite direction to the one before.

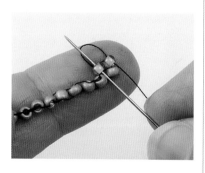

STEP 3
To neaten the start of your work, thread back through the first bead you added, then up through the second bead. This brings them closer together and stops the first bead from being too loose.

THREADING | OUT-BEAD
CROSS SECTION | START

Pick up two beads. Thread around the first thread loop on your ladder-stitch base and then back up your new bead.

Ladder the first two beads together to secure.

Brick stitch is transformed in this cuff by Lynn Davy, which features various-sized seed beads from size 11 to size 6 at random within an outline shape. This technique is known as freeform and doesn't have to be limited to brick stitch.

IN-BEAD START

STEP 1
As you bring the needle out of the end bead of your ladder-stitch base, pick up two beads. Thread under the loop of thread that separates the second and third beads in the base.

STEP 2
Thread back through the second bead you picked up, going in the opposite direction to the one before.

STEP 3
To neaten the start of your work, thread back through the first bead added, loop around the thread separating the first and second beads in the base, then thread back through the first bead added. (Skip this if your beads have small holes.)

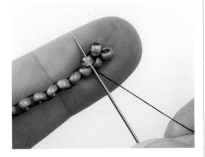

STEP 4
To get back in position to continue, thread down through the second bead added, loop around the thread separating the second and third beads in the base, then thread back through the second bead added.

THREADING CROSS SECTION | IN-BEAD START

Pick up two beads. Thread around the second thread loop on your ladder-stitch base and then back up your new bead.

Thread down through the first bead, around the first thread loop, and up the first bead. Repeat with the second bead.

A piece of tubular brick stitch (see page 112) can be wide enough to make a small purse, as on this necklace. Once beaded, the bottom edge was stitched together to make a usable pouch.

CONTINUING BRICK STITCH

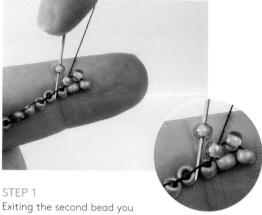

STEP 1

Exiting the second bead you added at the start, pick up one new bead. Thread around the next empty loop of thread on your ladder-stitch base. Then thread back up the new bead to finish the stitch.

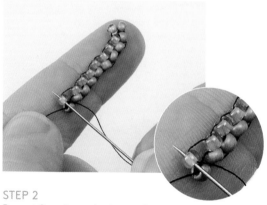

STEP 2

Repeat Step 1, continuing until you have no empty loops of thread left in the base.

THREADING CROSS SECTION	CONTINUING BRICK STITCH

Pick up one bead. Thread around the next empty thread loop on your ladder-stitch base, and then back up the new bead.

IN-BEAD FINISH

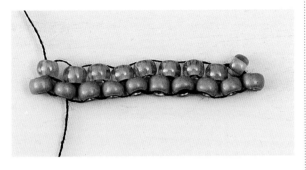

If you began with an out-bead start and want to keep your work the same width, you'll need to end with an in-bead finish. It's the simplest way to finish a row—stop once you've added a new bead to every loop on the base.

THREADING | IN-BEAD
CROSS SECTION | FINISH

Using brick stitch, add single beads to every thread loop in the ladder-stitch base.

CLINIC

FINDING A
REGULAR RHYTHM

- You may find it hard to keep your brick stitch rows straight and even, but persevere and practice until you find a comfortable way of holding your work and tensioning your thread.
- Gather all the supplies you need so you don't have to keep stopping and starting.
- Work slowly and gently, being careful not to split the thread loops when you pass under them with your needle. Draw the thread steadily through each bead, pulling just tight enough that there is no loose thread but not so tight that your beadwork is rigid.
- Some beads fit together more snugly than others and this can affect the tension. Cylinder beads have straight sides and will form a more closely woven texture than rounded seed beads.

OUT-BEAD FINISH

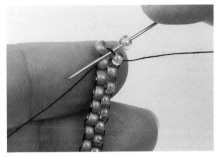

STEP 1
If you began with an in-bead start and want to keep your work the same width, you'll need to end with an out-bead finish. Begin by adding a new bead, but this time attach it to the same thread loop as the last bead added.

STEP 2
To neaten the end of the row and stop the extra bead from being too loose, ladder stitch it to the previous bead by circling through them both and pull tight.

THREADING | OUT-BEAD
CROSS SECTION | FINISH

Using brick stitch, add two beads to the last thread loop on the base.

Ladder-stitch the end two beads together for a neater finish and to secure the last bead.

continued →

TUBULAR BRICK STITCH

STEP 1

Begin with a ladder-stitch base with the ends joined. Pick up two beads and join the second one onto the closest empty thread loop. There is no need to secure the first bead you picked up.

STEP 2

Bead all around the base until there is just one empty thread loop left. You will now thread into the first bead, around the empty thread loop, and up the first bead. Repeat these steps until the tube is as long as needed.

THREADING | TUBULAR
CROSS SECTION | BRICK STITCH

Using brick stitch, begin a round on top of a ladder-stitch base with the ends joined. Continue until just one empty thread loop is left.

Using brick stitch, join the first bead picked up to the empty thread loop. Thread back through the bead and continue.

INCREASING AND DECREASING WITH BRICK STITCH

Increasing or decreasing at the edges of a flat piece of brick stitch is simply done by using out-bead starts and finishes. This adds extra beads to one, or both, sides. If you want to increase or decrease inside the body of your work, similar methods are used.

INCREASING WITHIN BRICK STITCH

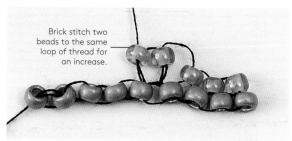

Brick stitch two beads to the same loop of thread for an increase.

STEP 1

Work brick stitch as you normally would. Then, at the point where you would like an increase, add an extra bead to the same loop of thread as the previous bead.

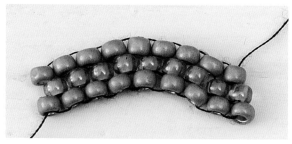

STEP 2

Continue beading as usual. When you reach the previous increase as you work the next round or row, add a bead onto each of the beads attached to the same loop.

THREADING | INCREASING WITHIN
CROSS SECTION | BRICK STITCH

To increase in the body of your work, add two beads, individually, to one thread loop.

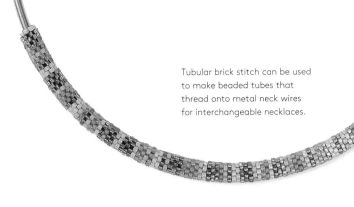

Tubular brick stitch can be used to make beaded tubes that thread onto metal neck wires for interchangeable necklaces.

DECREASING WITHIN BRICK STITCH

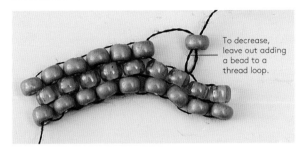

To decrease, leave out adding a bead to a thread loop.

STEP 1

Work brick stitch as you normally would. Then, at the point where you would like a decrease, add a bead to the next thread loop along (not to the next thread loop at the point of the decrease).

STEP 2

Continue beading as usual. When you reach the previous decrease as you work the next round or row, add a bead onto every thread loop.

THREADING | DECREASING WITHIN
CROSS SECTION | BRICK STITCH

To decrease in the body of your work, skip adding a bead to a thread loop and add the bead to the next loop along.

6 | SPECIAL FEATURES OF BRICK STITCH

- **Rotate brick stitch 90 degrees and it looks like peyote stitch.** It can sometimes be used as an alternative.

- **Brick stitch bends easily along its length**—but it won't bend across its width.

- **You can't achieve straight edges at the ends of rows.** This is because the ends are offset.

- **You can create straight lines and stripes along the width of a brick-stitch piece.** This is because the beads are offset from one row to the next—but you can't create them along the length.

- **A single bead centerpoint is easy to create in brick stitch.**

- **Hide the thread** by picking up two beads at the start of a row or round of brick stitch.

With its decoratively slanted beads, herringbone stitch is easy to learn and fast to bead. Once you've mastered turning, you'll soon see all the potential in this versatile technique.

Herringbone stitch

Herringbone stitch gets its name from the way the alternate beads in a row or round lie on a slant. This is an easily changeable stitch that produces a fluid piece of beadwork. A design bonus is that beads are added in pairs, which means it grows quickly! There are many ways to play with the basic stitch to decorate it. The instructions below should spark some creative ideas.

BEADING HERRINGBONE STITCH

This stitch is beaded adding multiples of two beads at a time (generally just two).

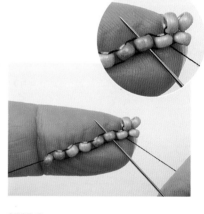

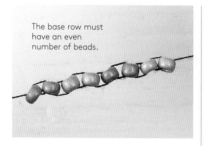

The base row must have an even number of beads.

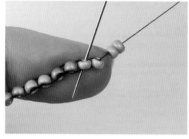

STEP 1
Begin with a strip of ladder stitch (see pages 106–107). It can be as wide as you like, but it must be made with an even number of beads. You may find it easier to bead this strip with pairs of alternating colors.

STEP 2
Pick up two beads (matching the last color used, if you are using alternate colors) and slide them down to your work. Thread down through the second bead from the end to join these new beads to the work.

STEP 3
Thread up through the next bead in your ladder-stitch base. This needs to be done every time, so that you are in the right position to continue.

THREADING | BEADING
CROSS SECTION | HERRINGBONE

Herringbone stitch is beaded by picking up two beads, threading down the next bead, then up the following bead.

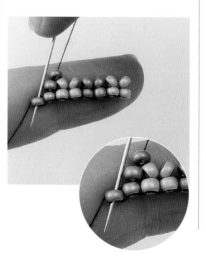

STEP 4
Pick up two beads (matching the next color in the row below) and slide them down to your work. Thread down through the second bead from where you are exiting.

STEP 5
Repeat Steps 3 and 4 until you have added as many pairs of beads as needed to cover the entire base strip. Finish after beading Step 4 so that you are exiting a bead in the base.

TURNING AT THE END OF A ROW

There are three different methods of turning at the end of a row of herringbone stitch, each of which takes you to the starting point of the next row. In each case, you need to have just added two new beads and be exiting a bead in your ladder-stitch base.

THREAD OUTSIDE

STEP 1
This is the easiest method. Simply take your needle and thread up the outside of the end bead in the row you are exiting, then thread into the last bead added.

WEAVE AROUND

STEP 1
This method is more intricate and can lead to the beads at the ends of your work sitting straight and losing their herringbone look. Take your needle and thread up the next bead toward the body of your work.

This colorful bracelet uses single beads added between the stacks (as in Step 1 of "Increasing between the stacks," page 119) to add extra color.

STEP 2
If you want to hide the thread and add a decorative twist to the turn, you can pick up a bead, or multiple small beads, before threading up the bead to turn.

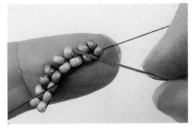

STEP 2
Thread through the bead above and over at the edge of your work. This is the last bead you added. You can now continue with the work.

LOOP AROUND

Exiting from a bead, take your needle and thread around the nearest thread loop before threading up the bead you are exiting and the last bead added.

THREADING | THREAD
CROSS SECTION | OUTSIDE TURN

Take your thread outside the edge bead and up the next bead.

THREADING | WEAVE
CROSS SECTION | AROUND TURN

Thread up the bead next to the one you are exiting, then thread up through the last bead added.

THREADING | LOOP
CROSS SECTION | AROUND TURN

Take your thread around the nearest thread loop, then thread back up the end bead.

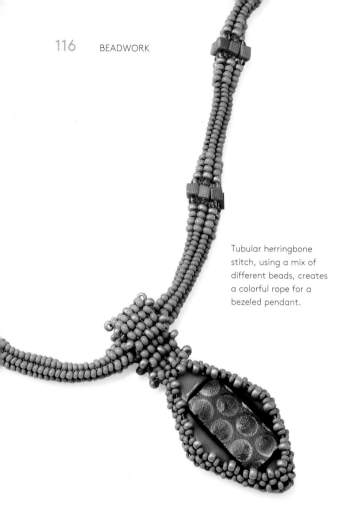

Tubular herringbone stitch, using a mix of different beads, creates a colorful rope for a bezeled pendant.

CONTINUING HERRINGBONE STITCH

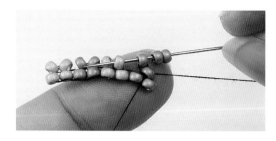

STEP 1
Pick up two beads to match the two beads at the end of the previous row. Thread down through the second bead in from the edge and up the third bead.

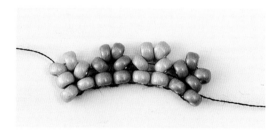

STEP 2
Repeat Step 1 until the row is fully beaded. Use the turn of your choice to continue.

TUBULAR HERRINGBONE STITCH

This is beaded in the same way as flat herringbone stitch, but with an added step-up at the end of the round instead of a turn.

THREADING | TUBULAR
CROSS SECTION | HERRINGBONE

At the end of every round of tubular herringbone stitch, you need to step up through one extra bead to be in the correct place to continue beading.

STEP 1
Begin with a strip of ladder stitch containing an even number of beads and joined at the ends. Pick up two beads, use herringbone stitch to attach them, and reposition.

STEP 2
Continue adding beads until there is just one stitch left. Pick up two beads and thread down through the appropriate bead to add them. Thread up the top two beads in the next stack to exit from a top bead. Continue beading.

SPIRALED HERRINGBONE STITCH

This is beaded in a similar way to tubular herringbone stitch, but with a change in the method that gives a twist to the final look. These instructions detail a simple "1 down, 2 up" method, but you can change the numbers for a less obvious or more pronounced spiral. You can also go down more and up less to turn the spiral in the other direction. It can take a few rounds for the twist to appear, so keep going.

STEP 1
Using tubular herringbone stitch, add one round to your base, making sure you step up at the end to reposition and prepare to continue.

STEP 2
Bead a round of tubular herringbone stitch. As you add the new beads, thread down through one bead in the appropriate stack and up the top two beads in the next stack.

STEP 3
Repeat threading down one bead and up two all the way around. Make sure to step up through three beads to finish the round and to exit the top bead in the next stack.

THREADING | SPIRALED
CROSS SECTION | HERRINGBONE STITCH

To make your herringbone tube spiral, you need to thread up and down different numbers of beads.

5 | DEFINING FEATURES OF HERRINGBONE STITCH

- **The beads in this stitch are meant to lie on a slant.** Be careful not to pull too tight to straighten them out.

- **Herringbone stitch is also known as Ndbele.** It is used in the traditional beadwork of the Ndbele people of South Africa.

- **You can bead stripes across the width and length, and even diagonally.** This is because the beads in this stitch lie directly next to and above each other.

- **Herringbone stitch is very flexible**—you can bend it gently in all directions.

- **Each stitch uses multiples of two beads.** If you want to bead 2-drop herringbone, for example, you'd need to pick up four beads per stitch.

INCREASING AND DECREASING IN HERRINGBONE STITCH

There are many methods and places for you to increase or decrease in herringbone stitch. The method you choose comes down to personal preference and whether you want to increase at the edges of your piece or within the body.

DECREASING AT THE EDGE

Don't add any beads to the last stacks.

This bracelet is beaded using 2-drop herringbone stitch (four beads picked up for each stitch, instead of the usual two). To add extra interest, drop beads were added between the two stacks (as in Step 2 of Increasing between the stacks, opposite).

Before you reach the end of your row, simply stop beading and adding new beads to decrease at the edge.

INCREASING AT THE EDGE

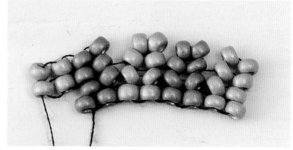

STEP 1
Once you have beaded a full row, use ladder stitch to add two new beads to the edge. If you have added the new beads to the last row, simply continue the next row.

STEP 2
If you have added the new beads to the second-to-last row beaded, you need to use herringbone stitch to add two new beads on top of them before you can continue.

INCREASING BETWEEN THE STACKS

STEP 1
When you reach the point where you want to increase, pick up two beads and thread down through the appropriate bead.

STEP 2
Pick up one new bead, then thread up the next bead in order to continue. If you want a quicker increase, you can skip this step and go on to the next one.

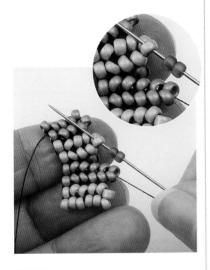

STEP 3
Bead the next row. When you reach the point where you've added the extra bead, add two new beads between the stacks as you did the single one. Bead the rest of the row as before.

STEP 4
Bead the next row. When you reach the extra beads, treat them as herringbone-stitched beads, threading up and down the beads as you would any other bead in the piece.

DECREASING WITHIN THE WORK

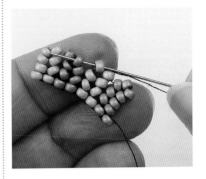

STEP 1
Bead herringbone stitch as needed. Then, when you reach the point where you want to decrease, thread through your work as you normally would, but with no beads on your thread.

STEP 2
If you find that leaving out beads gives you too big a gap, you can add one single bead to fill it.

STEP 3
Bead the next row as normal. When you reach it, ignore the decrease and thread up the next stack you added beads to. Continue beading.

Square stitch is an attractive stitch that, due to its construction, lends itself easily to pattern making and varied designs.

Square stitch

Square stitch could not be better named. Take advantage of its straight lines and grid-like nature to help you draw designs and patterns, and even use pictures and stitching patterns as inspiration for colorful pieces of beadwork. And because of the way the beads lie, square stitch lets you see where you are as you bead along.

Square stitch's natural affinity with stripes has been put to good use in the bracelet below to create a pattern of interweaving stripes.

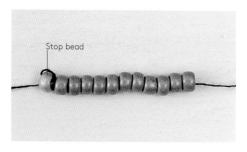

With a design inspired by a leaf, this bracelet shows how easily square stitch lends itself to pattern designing.

BEGINNING SQUARE STITCH

Stop bead

STEP 1
Add a stop bead to your thread, then pick up the number of beads you require for the width of your work. These beads form your first row.

STEP 2
Pick up one new bead (the first bead of your second row) and slide this down to your work. Circle through the last bead at the end of your first row to join them together, then through the new bead.

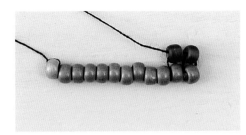

STEP 3

Pick up one new bead and slide this down to your work. Circle through the second-to-last bead at the end of your first row to join them together, then through the new bead.

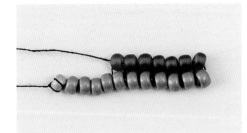

STEP 4

Continue adding new beads, securing each one to the bead directly under it and circling through the new bead, before continuing.

STEP 5

Once the whole row is beaded, you can weave through all the beads in the previous row, then all the beads in this row. Pull them more tightly together to secure your work.

STEP 6

Begin the next row as you did the second. Continue adding beads and rows, securing if desired, until your work is as long as you want.

THREADING CROSS SECTION | SQUARE STITCH

Square stitch is beaded by picking up a new bead, circling through the bead directly below to attach it, then through the new bead before continuing.

6 SPECIAL FEATURES OF SQUARE STITCH

- **This stitch gets its name from its grid-like pattern,** in which the beads sit squarely above and next to each other.

- **Square stitch can be used instead of beading on a loom.** The beads are arranged in exactly the same way as in loom work.

- **You can use cross-stitch and other grid-based sewing charts** to create designs for square stitch.

- **You can create straight lines in any direction in square stitch**—horizontally, vertically, and diagonally.

- **Square-stitch pieces bend easily across their width.** However, they do not bend along their length.

- **To speed up the stitch, pick up two beads at a time.** Then simply square stitch the second one onto the previous row.

continued ——▶

INCREASING AND DECREASING IN SQUARE STITCH

Square stitch allows you to add or remove beads easily at the edges while still keeping your work flat. Although increasing or decreasing within the body of a piece is straightforward, the work won't lie flat, so be prepared to incorporate this distinction into it.

DECREASING AT THE EDGES

To decrease at either edge, simply stop beading where you want to end, or just start further in from the end. Reduce the number of beads according to the size and shape you want.

THREADING CROSS SECTION | DECREASING AT THE EDGES

To decrease at an outside edge, you can either begin or end a row further in than the one below it.

INCREASING AT THE EDGES

STEP 1
You can increase at the start or end of any row. In the place where you want to increase, pick up as many extra beads as necessary to give you the width you want.

STEP 2
Square-stitch new beads on top of the new, additional beads to incorporate them into your work. If necessary, weave through the rows to neaten.

THREADING CROSS SECTION | INCREASING AT THE EDGES

To add extra beads at an outside edge, pick up as many beads as needed and then square stitch new beads onto them.

DECREASING WITHIN THE WORK

To decrease within your work, don't add a bead where you want the decrease to happen. Instead, attach your new bead to the next bead in your work.

THREADING CROSS SECTION | DECREASING WITHIN WORK

Once you reach the point where you want to decrease, skip the next bead in the row below and stitch your new bead to the next one along.

A bracelet by Norma Jean Dell in modified square stitch, netting, and right-angle weave, using two-holed beads and seed beads to frame an elegant line of glass pearls.

INCREASING WITHIN THE WORK

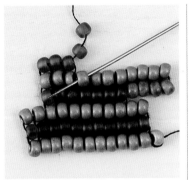

THREADING CROSS SECTION | INCREASING WITHIN WORK

When you reach the point where you want an increase, stitch two beads to the bead below instead of one.

STEP 1
To increase within your work, square stitch an extra bead to the bead in the row below so that it has two beads attached to it. You may find that the increase sits more naturally if you add the two beads in one stitch.

STEP 2
Bead the next row. When you reach the increase, square stitch a bead to each of those in the previous row.

TUBULAR SQUARE STITCH

STEP 1
Begin by picking up as many beads as necessary for the desired tube size. Join them into a circle by circling through some of the first beads you picked up.

STEP 2
Square stitch individual beads to those in your base row and circle through the new beads.

STEP 3
With each row, bead in the opposite direction. This is to be expected and not an error on your part!

Peyote is one of the most popular stitches, and it's fun to do. It can be tricky to start, but because it's a repeating pattern of creating spaces and filling them with beads, you'll get the rhythm in no time.

Peyote stitch

Depending on whether you want an obvious center to your work, you can bead either an odd- or even-count version of peyote stitch. This stitch can also be flat or tubular, creating very different effects. Both flat and tubular peyote are illustrated and explained over the following pages.

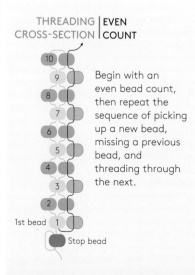

EVEN-COUNT FLAT PEYOTE

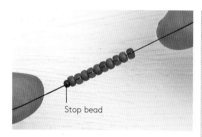

STEP 1
Add a stop bead to a length of thread, then pick up an even number of beads to match the width you want. Use alternating colors if you like. The initial beads that you have picked up sit in rows 1 and 2.

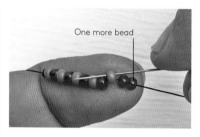

STEP 2
Pick up one more bead (the same as the last one added if you are using different colors). Thread your needle back through the second-to-last bead picked up in Step 1. If you are using two colors, you'll always thread into the one you're not adding.

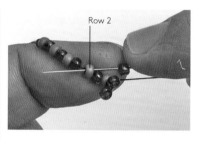

STEP 3
Pick up another new bead the same color as the last one. Missing the next bead of your beginning strand, thread through the next. What you're doing is missing the beads in row 1 and going through the ones in row 2 (see the diagram below).

STEP 4
Continue picking up one bead, missing one bead, and going through one bead all the way along your row. You will end up adding half as many new beads as in Step 1.

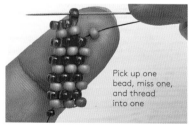

STEP 5
Continue as in Step 4. Soon your work will take shape. As you bead, you will see that you're creating the spaces that will fill in the next row.

THREADING CROSS-SECTION | EVEN COUNT

Begin with an even bead count, then repeat the sequence of picking up a new bead, missing a previous bead, and threading through the next.

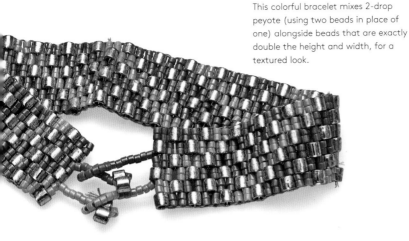

This colorful bracelet mixes 2-drop peyote (using two beads in place of one) alongside beads that are exactly double the height and width, for a textured look.

4 | WAYS TO TRACK WHERE YOU ARE

Counting how many rows you have beaded can be tricky, so here are four ways to check after finishing a row.

ODD-COUNT FLAT PEYOTE

STEP 1
Begin as in even-count peyote and stop when you're one bead from the end. You're now ready to perform the figure-8 turn that adds the last bead needed in row 3.

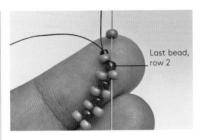

STEP 2
Thread through the last bead and pick up a bead. Then thread back diagonally through the second bead in from the edge of your work (the last bead in row 2) and the outside bead of the next pair (the second-to-last bead of row 1).

THREADING CROSS-SECTION | ODD-COUNT

This is based on even-count peyote but, at the end of alternate rows, you need to perform a figure-8 turn to add the last bead, then reposition.

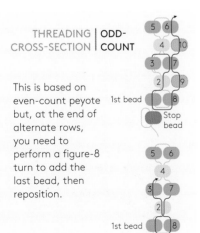

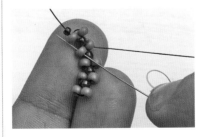

STEP 3
You have beaded three rows but need to reposition so that you can continue. Pass your needle and thread through the bead next to the one you are currently exiting, pointing toward the end of your row.

continued —→

COUNT BOTH SIDES
Count up the beads on both edges, then add the two figures together to get your total rows.

COUNT TWO COLUMNS
Identify any two columns next to each other and count the beads in each, adding them together to get your total number of rows.

COUNT ONE SIDE
Find the edge where the top bead sits lower than the other edge. Count along the edge, counting two for every bead. If at the end there's an extra lower row, just add this on for the total figure.

COUNT ON THE DIAGONAL
Identify the highest edge bead and count diagonally down your work until you reach the last bead. If you run out of beads, because of the shape of the piece, start again at the same side as you began.

TUBULAR PEYOTE STITCH

Taking peyote stitch tubular adds not just a whole new dimension but a lot of extra variety for you to play around with. The basics are the same as flat peyote but adding in an extra touch of difficulty with a step up or spiraling, so pay attention and soon you'll be tubing away!

EVEN-COUNT TUBULAR PEYOTE

Use a dowel for support.

STEP 1
Pick up an even number of beads for the size desired. Join into a circle by threading through one or more beads. It may help you to place your beadwork on a support such as a pen, bead tube, or dowel.

STEP 2
Pick up one new bead. Missing the next bead on your base circle, thread through the next. Continue this pattern of picking up one, missing one, and threading into one all the way around your base circle of beads.

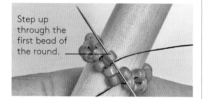

Step up through the first bead of the round.

STEP 3
Now you need to step up so that you are in the correct place to continue. Stitch through the first bead you added in this round so that you are exiting a higher bead.

STEP 4
Continue beading rounds, adding single beads into the higher beads (those added in the previous round) and stepping up at their end until your work is as long as desired.

ODD-COUNT TUBULAR PEYOTE

STEP 1
Begin as an even-count peyote, but this time pick up an odd number of beads in your base circle. Bead until you are just one bead from the end of your round.

No step-up; just keep adding single beads

STEP 2
This stitch doesn't have a step up, it just spirals around continuously. Simply carry on adding beads into the higher beads until your work is long enough.

CLINIC   COUNTING CLINIC

- Though it may look different, you can count your rounds in a similar way to how you counted the rows in flat peyote. The easiest method is counting two columns next to each other and adding the figures for the total. However, if your work is spiraling, you'll need to count on the diagonal.

CELLINI SPIRAL

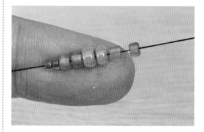

STEP 1
This version of even-count tubular peyote uses different sizes of beads for a textural effect. Begin by picking up pairs of beads in graduating sizes, for example, 2 x size 11, 2 x size 8, 2 x size 6, and 2 x size 8.

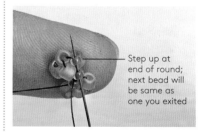

Step up at end of round; next bead will be same as one you exited

STEP 2
Thread through the first two beads to join into a circle. Begin beading peyote stitch, always picking up the same bead as the one you are exiting. At the end of the round, make sure to step up as usual.

INCREASING AND DECREASING IN PEYOTE

When beading peyote stitch, you can increase or decrease either at the edges or within the body of your work.

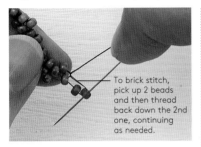

To brick stitch, pick up 2 beads and then thread back down the 2nd one, continuing as needed.

The last space has no bead added.

INCREASING AT THE EDGE
The simplest way to increase at the edges of your work is to bead your piece, then brick stitch from the loops of thread at the edges.

DECREASING AT THE EDGE
To decrease at an edge, simply stop beading when the row is the width you want, and change direction to begin the next row.

INCREASING WITHIN THE WORK

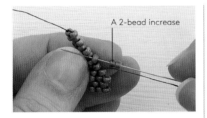

A 2-bead increase

Split the 2 beads with 1 bead to finish the increase.

STEP 1
Bead peyote stitch until you reach the point where the increase should occur. For the next stitch, pick up two beads instead of one.

STEP 2
When you reach the increasing point on the next row, split the two beads added in the previous row by adding one bead between them. Then bead the rest of the row as usual.

DECREASING WITHIN THE WORK

No bead on thread

STEP 1
Bead peyote stitch until you reach the point where you want the decrease. Then thread through your work as though you are still beading peyote for the next stitch, but with no bead on the thread.

STEP 2
When beading the next row, place one bead over the decrease and bead the rest of the row as normal.

---

6 | SPECIAL FEATURES OF PEYOTE STITCH

- **This stitch gets its name from Native American "peyote" ceremonies.** It was used to decorate objects in religious rituals.

- **Peyote stitch is also known as gourd stitch.**

- **You can make horizontal and diagonal stripes in peyote stitch.** Vertical stripes are not possible, because the beads are off-set from one another. Any stripes that run vertically across the width will zigzag.

- **Peyote stitch will bend along its width**—but it won't bend along its length.

- **Turned on its side, peyote stitch looks like brick stitch.** Use whichever stitch you prefer.

- **For designs with a single, central bead,** choose odd-count peyote stitch.

RAW may seem like a complicated stitch, but once you grasp its basic rules you'll soon be creating a piece of beadwork with a wonderful fabric drape.

Right-angle weave (RAW)

Though possibly the trickiest beading stitch to learn, right-angle weave—commonly known as RAW—involves some basic principles. Once you've learned these and understand the quirks of RAW, you'll be on your way to beading a stitch that is known for its fabric-like feel and drape, and its potential for embellishment and experimentation.

This bracelet uses RAW with a mix of different beads—in this case, seed and bugle beads for the floors and ceiling and seed beads for the walls.

BEGINNING RAW

Beading RAW is simply a matter of always trying to make groups of four beads. What makes it confusing is that you constantly change from beading in a clockwise to a counterclockwise direction. This alters from stitch to stitch and, while it doesn't matter so much for the first row, it means you have to pay special attention on subsequent rows.

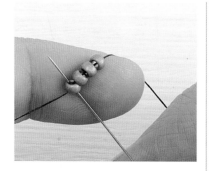

STEP 1
Add a stop bead to your thread, if desired, then pick up four seed beads. Circle through the first bead to join all four beads into a circle. This is your first box.

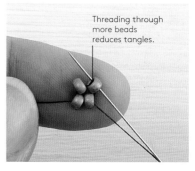

Threading through more beads reduces tangles.

STEP 2
You may now find it easier if you thread through one or two more beads. This will take you away from the bead where your tail thread is and will have no impact on your work (unless you're using a specific pattern of beads).

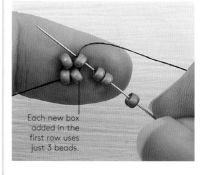

Each new box added in the first row uses just 3 beads.

STEP 3
Pick up three beads (this second box shares a wall with the first, so only three beads are needed to make a group of four). Circle through the bead you were exiting. Note whether you thread up or down the bead to go through it.

THREADING CROSS-SECTION | UNDERSTANDING RAW

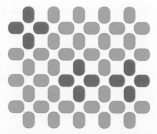

This diagram shows how your work will look if you used seed beads. The beads marked in red show some of the boxes within the work.

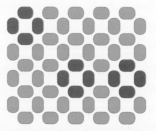

It is easier to understand the idea of boxes if you imagine the beads as being longer. The red beads are the same boxes as the first diagram.

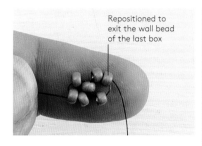

Repositioned to exit the wall bead of the last box

STEP 4

To reposition so that you can add more boxes, thread through two beads of the set of three added in Step 3. Note whether you had to thread clockwise or counterclockwise. This brings you out of the other wall bead on the second box.

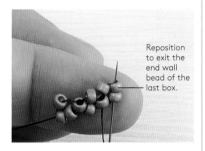

Reposition to exit the end wall bead of the last box.

STEP 6

Repeat Step 4 to weave through two beads and reposition to exit the other wall bead, ready to continue. This time you will weave in the opposite direction to Step 4—clockwise if you previously went counterclockwise, or vice versa.

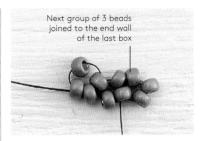

Next group of 3 beads joined to the end wall of the last box

STEP 5

Repeat Step 3 to add a new set of three beads to form your third group of four. This time you will circle through the bead already there in the opposite direction to Step 3—if you previously threaded down, you'll now thread up, or vice versa.

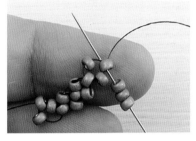

STEP 7

Repeat Steps 5 and 6, adding new sets of three beads to make new boxes, and repositioning to be ready to continue, until your work is as wide as desired. Remember that your weaving direction will alter from step to step.

THREADING CROSS-SECTION | BEGINNING THE 1ST ROW OF RAW

Begin with four beads joined in a circle. Then pick up three new beads, circle through the bead you were exiting, and weave through two beads to reposition and continue.

THREADING CROSS-SECTION | CONTINUING THE 1ST ROW OF RAW

Continue picking up three beads, circling through the bead you were exiting, and repositioning through two beads until your work is as long as desired.

THREADING CROSS-SECTION | UNDERSTANDING RAW

Box 3 shares its walls with Boxes 2 and 4.

The floor of Box 1 is the ceiling of Box 10 but its ceiling is its own as there are no boxes above it.

The ceiling of Box 13 is the floor of Box 8. Its floor is the ceiling of Box 18 and its walls are shared with Boxes 12 and 14.

This diagram shows a group of 20 boxes labeled in the order they are beaded.

Bead 3 is the floor of Box 1 and the ceiling of Box 10.

Bead 25 is the wall of both Boxes 10 and 9.

Bead 49 is the floor of Box 20 but not a ceiling as there is no box beneath it.

This diagram shows a group of 20 boxes, with each bead labeled in the order it was beaded.

THE COMPONENTS OF RAW

- **Floors and ceiling:** Each box has its own floor and ceiling, but it shares them with the boxes above and below, so the floor for one box is the ceiling for the one below.

- **Walls:** Each box has two walls—separated by the floor and ceiling—which it shares with the boxes to the left and right.

- **Sides:** All of the four components of the box can also be referred to as sides.

CONTINUING RAW

Once the first row of RAW is beaded, all subsequent rows are beaded the same. This time you will be adding either three beads each step (the first box of each new row) or two beads a step (all other boxes). The direction you need to thread and how many beads you need to thread through will depend on whether you added an odd or even number of boxes to your first row, as well as on the direction you thread when you first begin.

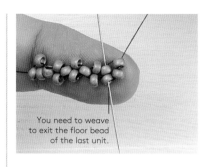
You need to weave to exit the floor bead of the last unit.

STEP 1
Before you can begin adding a new row, you need to get into the correct position. You want to be exiting the floor bead of your last box. If you are exiting your end wall bead facing upward, weave through three beads to exit the floor bead.

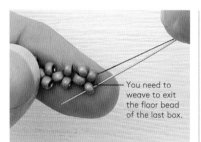
You need to weave to exit the floor bead of the last box.

STEP 2
If you are exiting the end wall bead facing down, then just weave through one bead to reposition and continue.

The first box of all subsequent rows needs 3 beads.

STEP 3
Pick up three new beads and circle through the floor bead you were exiting. This floor bead is now the ceiling bead of the box that you've just made.

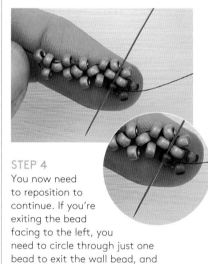

STEP 4
You now need to reposition to continue. If you're exiting the bead facing to the left, you need to circle through just one bead to exit the wall bead, and be ready to continue.

STEP 5
If you are exiting the bead facing to the right, then thread through four beads to weave around the box you just added. Then move on to exit the floor bead of the next box along in the previous row.

THREADING CROSS-SECTION | BEGINNING THE NEXT ROW OF RAW

Every time you begin a new row of RAW, you need to reposition your needle and thread so that you can exit the floor bead of the last box added, pick up three beads, and circle through the bead you were exiting. You then need to reposition so that you exit either the floor bead of the next box or the wall bead of the box you just made. Either way, you need to face in the direction in which you want to continue.

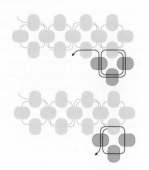

Each subsequent box of the second row onward needs just 2 beads added.

RULES OF RAW

- For each stitch, you are trying to make a group of four beads.

- You add all four beads only once, on the very first stitch. After this, you are adding either two or three beads to make up the four.

- Your stitching direction will vary from stitch to stitch. It will be either clockwise or counterclockwise.

- You never "leap" from one group of four to another. You always weave around until you exit a bead that sits in both the group you have just added and the next group that you want to bead.

- You need to get into position after you have added all the beads for a box, to enable you to continue beading.

STEP 6
Pick up two beads. Then, if you are exiting the wall bead, thread into the floor bead of the next box in the previous row. Now weave through four beads to get into position to exit the floor bead of the next box in the previous row.

STEP 7
If you are exiting the floor bead, thread into the wall bead of the box you previously added, and through two more beads to exit the wall bead just added.

STEP 8
Continue adding two beads for each new box. Alternate repositioning to exit either the wall bead of the box just added or the floor bead of the next box along in the row above.

STEP 9
When you begin the next row, you are back at Step 1 and need to get into position before picking up three beads to add the first box of this new row.

THREADING CROSS-SECTION | CONTINUING THE NEXT ROW OF RAW

Each stitch now needs just two beads to form the next box. After adding each new box, you need to alternate between weaving through four beads to exit the floor of the next box on the previous row and weaving through two beads to exit the wall bead of the box just added.

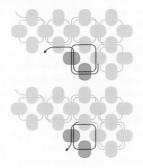

THE NUMBERS OF RAW

RAW is made up of a simple set of rules and numbers, and knowing these will make the stitch much easier to learn.

First row, first stitch: Pick up four beads.

First row, every other stitch: Pick up three beads.

Subsequent rows, first stitch: Pick up three beads.

Subsequent rows, every other stitch: Pick up two beads.

INCREASING AND DECREASING IN RAW

When beading RAW, you can increase or decrease either at the edges of your work or within the body of what you're beading.

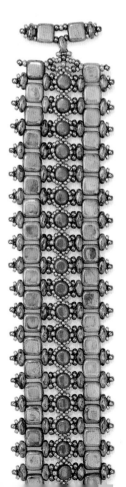

Norma Jean Dell's "Painted way" bracelet uses RAW and netting to bring together a variety of shaped and two-hole beads.

TUBULAR RAW

STEP 1
Bead your first row of RAW and join the ends together by just adding the floor and ceiling beads of the last box, as the walls are already there.

STEP 2
Weave so that you exit any of the ceiling beads in the row just added. Continue beading tubular RAW as you do regular RAW, although now the last box of each round only needs one bead added to make the group of four.

DECREASING AT THE EDGE

Leave as many boxes as desired unbeaded at the end of your row.

Simply stop beading RAW and adding new boxes before you reach the end of your row to decrease at that edge.

INCREASING AT THE EDGE

This is equivalent to beading your first-row boxes. You need to pick up groups of three beads and reposition to add as many extra boxes to the side as desired.

This "Gritty tweed" bracelet by Norma Jean Dell combines two-hole Superduo beads with seed beads in a modified RAW stitch.

7 | KEY POINTS ABOUT RAW

- **Beads within RAW lie at right angles to each other**—hence the name.

- **A piece of RAW can be bent and folded in any direction.** This makes it the ideal piece of beadwork to drape or cover something.

- **Just like other stitches, RAW can be two- or more-drop.** Simply pick up two beads instead of one for each "side" that you're beading.

- **RAW allows you to mix drops.** This is because you're always picking up beads for the length and width as you bead. You could decide to have two beads for every ceiling and floor and just one bead for each wall. As long as you keep it consistent, your work will be even.

- **RAW allows you to mix bead shapes and sizes.** As with mixing drops, you could use long bugle beads for the "ceilings" and "floors" and small seed beads for the walls.

- **The beads in a piece of RAW catch the light differently** because they lie with their holes both horizontally and vertically—and the same bead or finish can look different depending on whether it was used for a wall or ceiling/floor.

- **The lines within RAW are straight,** so you can have stripes made of boxes, beads across the length and width, or boxes diagonally across the work.

DECREASING WITHIN THE WORK

Attach your new box to 2 boxes in the previous row.

When you reach the spot where you want to decrease, you can simply skip adding a box to the next box along in the previous row. Alternatively, for a neater finish, attach your new box to the floor beads of the next two boxes in the previous row.

INCREASING WITHIN THE WORK

Pick up 3 beads instead of 2.

STEP 1

When you reach the point where you want to add an increase, pick up an extra bead for the next box and bead so that the floor of this box has two beads.

3 WAYS TO ACHIEVE SUCCESS WITH RAW

- **Relax!** Don't worry too much if, for example, you skip across an intersection—as long as you have the basic stitch right, no one will notice small errors.

- **Look closely.** Always look at what you're beading and soon you'll be able to clearly see what's happening and where you are in the sequence.

- **Count to 4.** Look at the group you're beading into and count how many beads are already there. Then all you have to do is make sure that it adds up to four.

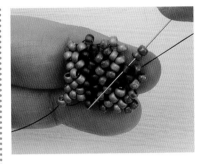

STEP 2

Bead the next row. When you reach the spot where you previously increased, add a new box onto each of the floor beads of the box above.

This clever relative of RAW is an effective technique for creating three-dimensional pieces of beadwork and striking pieces of jewelry.

Cubic right-angle weave (CRAW)

Cubic right-angle weave, also known as CRAW, is easier to learn than right-angle weave. Like RAW, it has a simple repetitive pattern, but with this stitch you can break many of the rules of RAW and have fun.

RUNNING ORDER

First step: Pick up four beads.

Every round, 1st stitch: Pick up three beads, weave through two.

Every round, 2nd stitch: Pick up two beads, weave through three.

Every round, 3rd stitch: Pick up two beads, weave through four.

Every round, 4th stitch: Pick up one bead, weave through four beads to continue.

BEADING CRAW

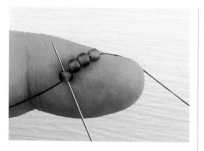

STEP 1
Base circle: On a length of thread, pick up four beads and circle through the first one to join into a circle. These will be the floor beads of the four boxes you'll add in the first round.

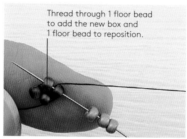

Thread through 1 floor bead to add the new box and 1 floor bead to reposition.

STEP 2
First box: Pick up three beads (wall, ceiling, and wall) and circle through the bead you are exiting. To reposition, move on to the next bead in the base circle (floor).

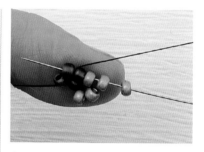

STEP 3
Second box: Pick up two beads (wall and ceiling) and circle through the first bead added in Box 1 (a wall bead) and the bead you were exiting (floor). To reposition, weave through the next bead on the base circle (floor).

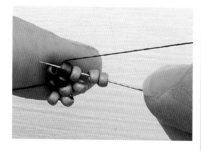

STEP 4
Third box: Pick up two beads (wall and ceiling) and circle through the first bead added in Box 2 (wall) and the bead you are exiting (floor).

STEP 5
Fourth box: You need to add only one bead for this. To reposition so you can do this, thread through the next bead in the base circle (floor) and the third bead picked up in Box 1 (wall).

THREADING | BEADING
CROSS-SECTION | CRAW

Begin with four base beads joined into a circle (these are your floor beads and are shown in blue). To bead the first box, pick up three beads and circle through the floor bead you were exiting and the next one along.

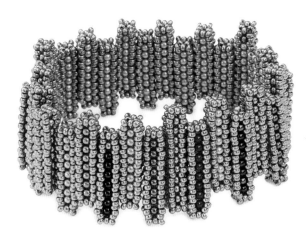

This bracelet is formed of multiple strips of CRAW made using seed beads and pearls strung together with beading elastic.

3 | DEFINING FEATURES OF CRAW

- **To understand CRAW, imagine that you are beading six-sided cubes, one sitting on top of the next.** The stitch is designed to be beaded in lengths formed of four boxes/sides.

- **You can choose the direction you work in.** In RAW, you alternate stitching clockwise and counterclockwise. In CRAW, you can choose your direction after every round.

- **The base circle is only beaded once.** After that, it's the basic pattern of adding four boxes.

STEP 6

Last box: This needs only its ceiling added. Pick up one bead and thread into the first bead added in Box 3 (wall). To reposition so that you can bead the next round, weave through the floor, the wall of Box 1, and the ceiling of Box 1.

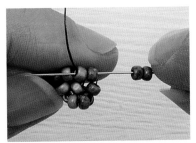

STEP 7

Repeat Steps 2–6 to add rounds of four boxes directly on top of each other. The ceiling you added in the previous round will now be the floor beads you weave through to add beads and reposition.

To bead the second box, pick up two beads. Circle through the wall of the first box, the floor of this new box, and the next floor along.

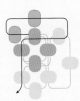

To bead the third box, pick up two beads. Circle through the wall of the second box, the floor of this new box, and the next floor along. Then thread through the wall of the first box ready to add the last box.

To bead the fourth box, pick up one bead. Circle through the wall of the third box, the floor of this new box, the wall of the first box, and the ceiling of the first box. You are now ready to begin the next round.

Working with a loom allows you to create beadwork with a fabric-like feel in record time. Choose your finishing method carefully and you won't have to worry about weaving away all those warp threads.

Loom work

Loom work is the only beading technique that needs a piece of equipment. The name of the technique comes from that essential tool: a loom. Once set up, the actual beading process can go rather quickly. Although many people are put off by all the thread ends to weave away, using a different finishing method (pulled warps) makes loom work easy.

WARPING YOUR LOOM

There are lots of different ways to warp your loom. Using the continuous warps method allows you to use either of the two methods of looming and finishing. It also lets you change what method you use.

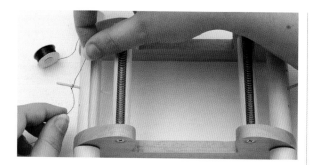

STEP 1
Working straight from your reel of thread, tie one end to the peg or screw on your loom. Then work out how many warp threads you need (the number of beads you want in your width, plus one) and halve this number.

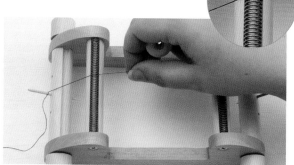

STEP 2
Find the central groove on one of your coils. Using the halved number, count that many grooves from the center. Lay your thread so it sits in that groove.

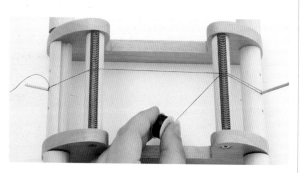

STEP 3
Take your thread along the length of your loom and find the corresponding groove in the other coil. Lay the thread in this groove, then wrap it around the peg at the end and lay it in the next groove.

STEP 4
Repeat Step 3 until you have added the number of warp threads needed in Step 1. Tie the end of the thread to the peg or use sticky tape to attach it to the roller.

The straight strips produced with loomwork are ideal for bracelets. Make them wide or narrow by changing the number of warp threads you use. You can find special beading graph paper online for charting your patterns.

You can buy beading looms in many different sizes that enable you to vary the size of your beadwork. There are some basic components that all these looms feature. They will all have rollers with pegs, screws, or holes for toothpicks to which you can attach your warp threads and make longer pieces of beadwork if needed. They will also have wire coils to hold your warp threads in order to separate them and make it easier for you to add your beads.

8 THINGS YOU SHOULD KNOW ABOUT LOOM WORK

- **Warp threads are the threads attached to your loom and what you weave onto.**

- **The threads that the beads sit on are your weft threads.**

- **Use loom work and square stitch interchangeably.** The two stitches resemble each other.

- **Create designs from cross-stitch and other grid-based sewing charts.** The beads sit squarely in loom work, so the structure is similar to that of grid-based stitching.

- **Loomed pieces can have straight lines and stripes in every direction**—across the width and length, as well as diagonally.

- **Loom work bends easily across its width.** It does not bend easily across its length.

- **If the grooves in your coil are too close for the size of bead, use every other groove.** Alternatively, skip the necessary number to accommodate the width of your beads.

- **Pick up beads in batches for wider beadwork.** Lay them under your warp thread, and thread back through in groups.

BEGINNING TO LOOM

When looming, you'll add groups of beads on weft threads and attach them to your warp threads. Exactly how you loom and add new threads will depend on whether you wish to weave away your thread ends or use the pulled warps method (see opposite) to finish. Add a needle to your thread.

Weave away: Cut each warp thread and weave them into your work individually to secure. For this method, you can knot warp threads on to your wefts to secure them and not worry about weaving back and forth through your work or splitting threads.

Pulled warps: Beginning at the center of your work, gently pull the warp threads through your work so you finish with just two ends to weave away. Make sure not to split your warp threads, tie any knots, or weave unnecessarily through your work. Once you've finished, weave all weft threads into your work.

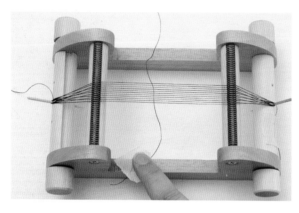

STEP 1
To begin a weft thread, knot it onto an edge warp thread (weave-away method) or use sticky tape to attach it to the loom (pulled-warps method).

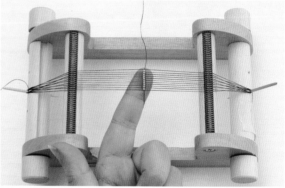

STEP 2
Pick up the beads you need for your first row and place your thread under the warp threads. Separate the beads so that each one sits between its own warp threads—this will get easier as you continue.

STEP 3
Take your weft thread back through all the beads, this time making sure you thread over the warp threads. Avoid splitting your warp threads by pushing your needle eye first through the beads.

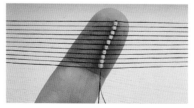

STEP 4
Slide your beads up and down your warp threads to make sure the threads haven't split. If there are any split warps, undo this row and start again. (If you're planning on weaving your threads away, you don't need to do this.)

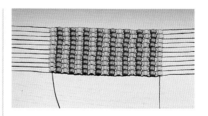

STEP 5
Continue adding rows of beads until you have beaded all of your work. Any time you need to finish or add a thread, just weave it through your work and knot it to the warps (weave-away method) or tape it to your loom (pulled-warps method).

FINISHING YOUR LOOM WORK

There are two methods to finish your work: weaving threads away and pulled warps. Which one you choose is up to you.

WEAVING THREADS AWAY

STEP 1
Cut the loops off the ends of all your threads and weave each one individually into your work to secure and finish them.

STEP 2
If you want to add a clasp to your work, weave the ends to the center of each side, tie them into a knot, trim, then add a clamshell (see page 43) over the knot to attach.

PULLED WARPS

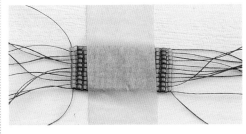

STEP 1
Carefully remove your work from your loom (don't cut the threads). Tape it down to your work surface. This will help you to avoid distorting your threads when you pull the warps.

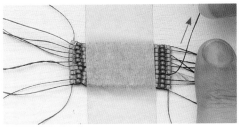

STEP 2
Beginning near the center-right end of your work, gently pull on a warp thread loop until it has pulled all the way from the left.

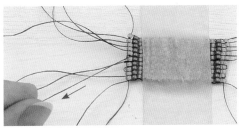

STEP 3
Move on to the next warp thread at the left end of your work and gently pull until it comes all the way through from the right.

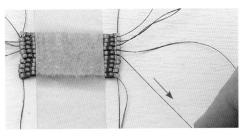

STEP 4
Continue pulling warps until the side is finished. Go back to the center of your work and pull the other side. If you pierce any threads or a warp won't pull, simply move on to the next—you'll just have an extra thread to weave in.

STEP 5
To add a clasp at the center, pull some of the warps at the ends and take the long lengths in the center. Tie them in a knot, trim, and add a clamshell over the knot on which to secure a clasp.

Turning crystals and cabochons into beautiful pendants, centerpieces, and eye-catching jewelry is easy once you know the basics of bezeling.

Bezeling

When bezeling a cabochon, your aim is to hold it securely and neatly while keeping the front on display. Fortunately, modern cylinder beads and crystals are perfectly sized so that exact formulas can be given for bezeling in peyote stitch. Even odd-shaped cabochons can be bezeled using different stitches. With some experimentation, you'll soon be able to show off these special stones within your own design.

This agate slice is bezeled using peyote stitch and a mix of seed beads.

THE BASICS OF BEZELING

Whichever stitch you choose, your beadwork should be the same size, but slightly deeper, than the size of your cabochon. You then want to decrease the beadwork, through decreasing stitches or smaller beads, so that it covers the edge at the front and back and holds your piece securely.

USING RAW AND PEYOTE STITCH

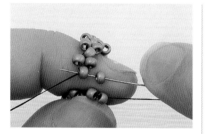

STEP 1
Bead a strip of RAW that fits all around your cabochon and is slightly deeper. You may need to think carefully about the size of the beads to use, or add more than one round. Join the ends of the strip together.

STEP 2
Exit a ceiling bead and begin peyote stitch (using different beads and adding more than one bead or no beads per space if necessary). Thread from ceiling bead to ceiling bead. Add extra rounds if necessary. Insert the cabochon and repeat the process at the back.

This beaded flower pendant has a 30mm flatback chessboard crystal (see bezeling formula on page 143) as its centerpiece.

USING TUBULAR PEYOTE STITCH

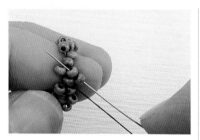

STEP 1
Join a number of beads into a circle. An even number of beads will make this easier, because you want the circle to fit around the outside edge of your cabochon. Using even-count peyote stitch, bead until the piece is slightly deeper than your cabochon.

STEP 2
Switch to smaller beads (or decreasing stitches) to decrease your work inward. Bead as many rounds as needed until the piece will hold your cabochon. Insert your cabochon and repeat the process at the back of your work.

THREADING | CRYSTAL BEZELING
CROSS-SECTION | FORMULAS

The patterns below work in peyote stitch with Swarovski crystals,
size 15 seed beads, and size 11 cylinder beads.

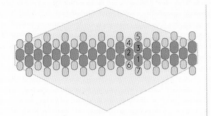

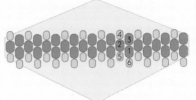

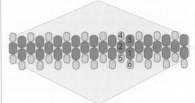

BEZELING A 14MM RIVOLI

Rounds 1–2: Thread your needle with a workable length of thread. Pick up 36 cylinder beads and circle through the first two to join into a circle, leaving a long tail thread.

Round 3: Bead a round using one cylinder bead in every space. Make sure you step up to end the round by exiting the first bead added.

Rounds 4–5: Bead two rounds using one seed bead in every space, ensuring you pull tight so your work decreases.

Rounds 6–7: Return to your tail thread and, at the back of your work, add one round using one seed bead in every space. Insert your crystal so that it faces out through Rounds 4–5, then bead one more round using one seed bead in every space.

BEZELING A 12MM RIVOLI

Rounds 1–2: Thread your needle with a workable length of thread. Pick up 30 cylinder beads and circle through the first two to join into a circle, leaving a long tail thread.

Round 3: Bead a round using one cylinder bead in every space. Make sure you step up to end the round by exiting the first bead added.

Round 4: Bead a round using one seed bead in every space. Make sure you step up to end the round by exiting the first bead added, then weave through this round a few times to secure the work.

Rounds 5–6: Return to your tail thread and, at the back of your work, add one round using one seed bead in every space. Insert your crystal so that it faces out through Round 4, then bead one more round using one seed bead in every space.

BEZELING A 10MM RIVOLI

Rounds 1–2: Thread your needle with a workable length of thread. Pick up 26 cylinder beads, and circle through the first two to join into a circle, leaving a long tail thread.

Round 3: Bead a round using one cylinder bead in every space. Make sure you step up to end the round by exiting the first bead added.

Round 4: Bead a round using one seed bead in every space. Make sure you step up to end the round by exiting the first bead added, then weave through this round a few times to secure the work.

Rounds 5–6: Return to your tail thread and, at the back of your work, add one round using one seed bead in every space. Insert your crystal so that it faces out through Round 4, then bead one more round using one seed bead in every space.

BEZELING RIVOLIS

These gorgeous Swarovski crystals are easy to bezel and add just the right amount of sparkle. Check the diameter to make sure you apply the right bezeling formula.

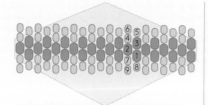

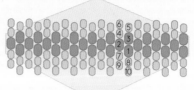

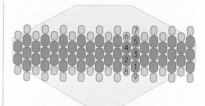

BEZELING A 16MM RIVOLI

Rounds 1–2: Thread your needle with a workable length of thread. Pick up 42 cylinder beads and circle through the first two to join into a circle, leaving a long tail thread.

Round 3: Bead a round using one cylinder bead in every space. Make sure you step up to end the round by exiting the first bead added.

Rounds 4–6: Bead three rounds, using one seed bead in every space. Make sure you step up to end the rounds.

Rounds 7–9: Return to your tail thread and, at the back of your work, add two rounds using one seed bead in every space. Insert your crystal so that it faces out through Rounds 4–6, then bead one more round using one seed bead in every space.

BEZELING AN 18MM RIVOLI

Rounds 1–2: Thread your needle with a workable length of thread. Pick up 46 cylinder beads and circle through the first two to join into a circle, leaving a long tail thread.

Round 3: Bead a round using one cylinder bead in every space. Make sure you step up to end the round by exiting the first bead added.

Rounds 4–6: Bead three rounds, using one seed bead in every space. Make sure you step up to end the rounds.

Rounds 7–10: Return to your tail thread and, at the back of your work, add two rounds using one seed bead in every space. Insert your crystal so that it faces out through Rounds 4–6, then bead one more round using one seed bead in every space.

BEZELING A SWAROVSKI 27MM ROUND STONE

Rounds 1–2: Thread your needle with a workable length of thread. Pick up 64 beads and join into a circle by threading through two beads, leaving a long tail thread.

Round 3–5: Using cylinder beads, add another three rounds of peyote stitch.

Rounds 6–7: Using seed beads, add two rounds of peyote stitch, ensuring you pull tight so that the work decreases.

Rounds 8–9: Return to your tail thread and repeat Rounds 6–7. As you work, insert your crystal into your bezel at a suitable point so that it is held tightly within your beadwork.

This bangle uses an eye-catching 30mm crystal (see "Bezeling a 30mm round flatback stone Swarovski #2035 chessboard," opposite) attached to a metal bangle base covered in RAW.

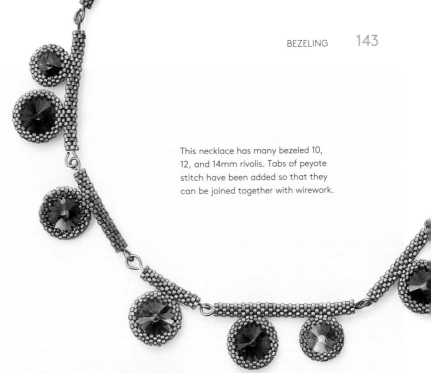

This necklace has many bezeled 10, 12, and 14mm rivolis. Tabs of peyote stitch have been added so that they can be joined together with wirework.

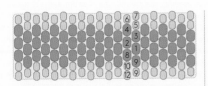

BEZELING A 30MM ROUND FLATBACK STONE SWAROVSKI #2035 CHESSBOARD I

Rounds 1–2: Thread your needle with a workable length of thread. Pick up 72 cylinder beads and join into a circle by threading through two beads, leaving a long tail thread.

Rounds 3–4: Using cylinder beads, add two rounds of peyote stitch.

Rounds 5–7: Using seed beads, add three rounds of peyote stitch, ensuring you pull tight so the work decreases.

Rounds 8–12: Return to your tail thread and repeat Rounds 3–7. As you work, insert your crystal into your bezel at a suitable point so that it is held tightly within your beadwork.

BEZELING A 20MM ROUND FLATBACK STONE—THE SMALLER VERSION OF SWAROVSKI #2035

Rounds 1–2: Thread your needle with a workable length of thread. Pick up 48 cylinder beads and join into a circle, leaving a long tail thread.

Rounds 3–5: Using cylinder beads, add three rounds of circular peyote stitch.

Rounds 6–7: Using seed beads, add two rounds of circular peyote stitch, pulling tight so that the work decreases.

Rounds 8–9: Return to your tail thread and add two rounds using seed beads. Insert your crystal into your bail as you work, at a suitable point, so it is held tightly within your beadwork.

Quick start project:

Bubbles bracelet

Begin building your beadwork jewelry collection with this fun peyote stitch bracelet that uses different bead combinations to create texture.

MATERIALS AND TOOLS

- 8g x size 8 seed beads
- 10g x 4mm magatama drop beads or similar
- Clasp
- Scissors
- Beading needle
- Beading thread

TECHNIQUE See also:
- Peyote stitch (page 124)

BEADING THE BRACELET

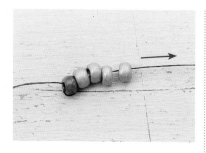

STEP 1
Using a workable length of thread, add a stop bead to the end, then pick up four seed beads. These are the first two rows of your bracelet.

STEP 2
Now change direction and work back to bead the third row. Pick up one drop bead. Skipping the last seed bead picked up, thread through the next one.

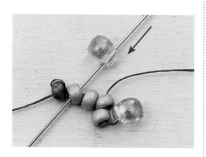

STEP 3
Pick up one more drop bead. Skipping the next seed bead that you picked up in Step 1, thread through the next one. You've now beaded the third row of your bracelet.

STEP 4
Now change direction and bead the fourth row of your bracelet. Pick up one seed bead and thread through the last drop bead added.

STEP 5
Pick up one more seed bead. Skipping the next seed bead, thread though the drop bead that you picked up in Step 2. You've now beaded the fourth row of your bracelet. Add another row, using seed beads for your fifth row.

STEP 6
Repeat Steps 2–5 until your work is as long as desired (minus the clasp length). Finish with a seed bead row to neaten the end.

STEP 7
Weave to exit the seed bead that is one in from the edge on the second-to-last row added. Make sure you exit it facing toward the closest edge.

STEP 8
Begin the next row by adding one seed bead. Then change direction to begin another row. Pick up one seed bead and thread into the last seed bead added. You've now added two rows of just one bead each.

STEP 9
Pick up two seed beads, followed by your clasp. Thread back through the seed beads and weave your thread into your work to secure and finish.

STEP 10
Return to your tail thread and repeat Steps 7–8 at this end to add the other end of the clasp and finish the bracelet.

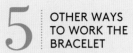

5 OTHER WAYS TO WORK THE BRACELET

- **Use herringbone or brick stitch** to bead a similar piece.

- **Pick up more beads from the beginning** to make a wider bracelet.

- **Make a bangle instead of a bracelet.** Rather than adding a clasp, "zip" the ends of your peyote stitch together. To do this, make sure you begin with a strip of peyote stitch with an even number of rows. Bring the edges together and weave from one edge to the other, threading through the beads that stick out.

- **Replace the drops with dagger beads** to add extra texture.

- **Cover your thread with French wire** to protect it from rubbing on the clasp.

Guest Designer SHONA BEVAN

66 I love to create a big impact with tiny beads, and I make elegant, wearable jewelry with a focus on beautiful finishing. After building up a strong repertoire of beading stitches, I began teaching my own designs in 2013, and now teach regularly throughout England, UK. 99

Trellis bracelet

This statement bracelet has an open lattice design constructed in cubic right-angle weave (CRAW) and accented with Swarovski pearls and crystals.

MATERIALS AND TOOLS

- 10g x size 11 Miyuki round seed beads (main color: MC)
- 10g x size 11 Miyuki round seed beads (contrast color: CC)
- 40 x 3mm Swarovski Elements Pearls 5810
- 72 x 3mm Swarovski Elements Bicones 5328
- 2 x 6mm jump rings
- 1 x magnetic clasp
- 6lb Fireline in smoke-gray or crystal-white
- Size 12 beading needle
- Scissors or thread burner
- 2 pairs flat-nose pliers

TECHNIQUES See also:

Opening and closing jump rings, page 64
CRAW, page 134

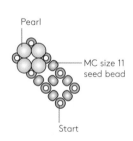

Pearl

MC size 11 seed bead

Start

STEP 1

Make one CRAW cube (see page 134) with main-color (MC) beads. Start the next cube with one MC bead, a 3mm pearl, and more MC beads. Complete the cube with MC beads. End the cube with your thread coming out of the pearl. Start the next cube with three pearls, then complete the cube with MC beads.

STEP 2

Rotate your work by 90° and make two cubes with MC beads. The new cubes will be at right angles to the previous ones and the pearls will be at the corner. Start the next cube with one MC bead, one bicone, and an additional MC bead, then complete the cube with MC beads. End the cube with your thread coming out of the bicone. Make sure that the bicone sits on the same side of the work as the pearls. Start the next cube with three bicones, then complete the cube with MC beads.

BEADER'S WISDOM

● ● ●

A nine-diamond bracelet using size 11 beads is 1 in (2.5cm) wide and will fit an average-sized wrist of 7¹/₂ in (19.5cm). For a smaller wrist, make the bracelet with just eight diamonds; for a larger wrist, try 10 or 11 diamonds.

● ● ●

If you prefer bangles to bracelets, you can connect the ends of your Trellis together instead of adding a clasp. You will need more diamonds for a bangle than for a bracelet, so remember to try on your bangle for size before you embellish the edges or finish off any threads.

FINISHED SIZE
1 in (2.5cm) wide, will fit an average-sized wrist of 7¹/₂ in (19.5cm)

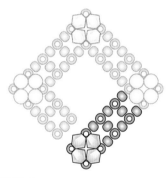

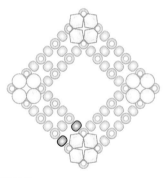

STEP 3
Rotate your work by 90° and make two cubes with MC beads. Start the next cube with one MC bead, one pearl, and an additional MC bead, then complete the cube with MC beads. End the cube with your thread coming out of the pearl. Start the next cube with three pearls, then complete the cube with MC beads.

STEP 4
Rotate your work by 90° and make two cubes with MC beads. Start the next cube with one MC bead, one bicone, and an additional MC bead, then complete the cube with MC beads. End the cube with your thread coming out of the bicone. Start the next cube with three bicones, then complete the cube with MC beads.

STEP 5
Connect the last cube to the first cube using MC beads, then position your thread so that it is coming out of a pearl on the outside edge of the diamond, ready to start the next diamond.

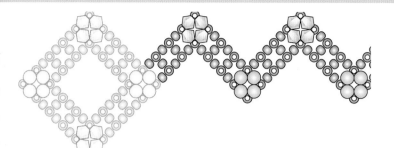

STEP 6

Repeat Steps 2 and 3 eight times. Make sure you turn the beadwork in opposite directions between each step to create a zigzag effect.

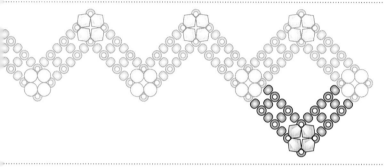

STEP 7

Repeat Step 2, then rotate your work by 90° and make two cubes with MC beads. Connect the last cube to the next pearl-topped cube to complete the diamond.

STEP 8

Repeat Step 7 along the length of the bracelet to complete all the diamonds.

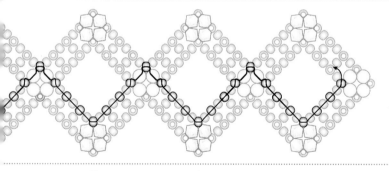

STEP 9

Weave around the inside edge of the front of the bracelet, following a zigzag path from one end to the other and back again, adding one contrast-color (CC) size 11 bead in each space. The zigzag thread path is more straightforward than embellishing the inside of each diamond individually.

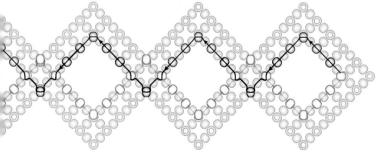

STEP 10

Repeat Step 9 to embellish the inside edge of the back of the bracelet.

Shona Bevan

4 GREAT VARIATIONS YOU CAN TRY

- Experiment with bead sizes and the placement of your accent beads.
- Replacing the pearls with crystals will give you added sparkle.
- Using size 8 seed beads and 4mm accent beads will give your trellis a much chunkier look.
- Adding extra rows is another good way to add more drama to this statement bracelet.

STEP 11

Weave around the outside edge of all the diamonds on the front of the bracelet, adding one CC bead in each space along the sides of each diamond and three CC beads at each point.

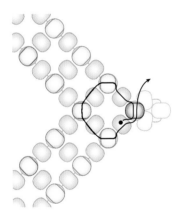

STEP 12

Weave around the outside edge of the back of the bracelet, adding one CC bead in each space until you reach the corner unit at the end of the bracelet. Pick up one CC bead, then weave through the four seed beads on the back of this unit again, and step up through the size 11 bead just added.

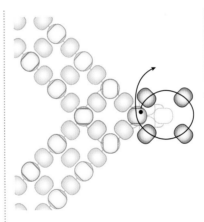

STEP 13: CLASP LOOP

Pick up four CC beads and pass through the bead you started from in the same direction as before. Repeat the thread path to reinforce, then step up through the first bead added.

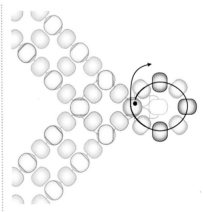

STEP 14

Pick up one CC bead and pass through the next bead in the loop. Repeat twice more, then pass through all the beads in the loop again to reinforce. Continue embellishing the outside edge of the back of the bracelet, remembering to add a second clasp loop when you reach the other end of the bracelet. Finish off all threads.

STEP 15

Using jump rings, connect your clasp to the loops at each end of the bracelet.

Guest Designer KERRIE SLADE

" I have been beading for over 12 years, and have had work published in numerous books and magazines around the world. I have taught beadwork internationally and sell my patterns via my website at www.kerrieslade.co.uk. You can visit my blog at kerrieslade.blogspot.com. "

Brick stitch bloom

Create this beautiful blooming brooch by mixing two-drop and single-drop brick stitch to form a realistic-looking flower.

MATERIALS AND TOOLS

- 5g x size 10 seed beads in color A (Preciosa Ornela 331 19001 63021 green)
- 12g x size 10 seed beads in color B (Preciosa Ornela 331 19001 46025 purple)
- 1 x 8mm glass pearl (white or cream)
- Beading thread to match your chosen beads (6lb Fireline in smoke)
- 1½ in (36mm) round sieve brooch finding
- Scissors
- Size 10–12 beading needle
- Flat-nose pliers

TECHNIQUES See also:

Ladder stitch, page 106
Brick stitch, page 108

STEP 1

Thread a needle with 35 in (90cm) of thread and pick up four color A beads. Leaving a 10-in (25-cm) tail, ladder stitch them together so that two stacks of two beads sit side by side. Pass your needle through all the beads again so that they are locked tightly together.

STEP 2

Begin working in increasing two-drop brick stitch and pick up four color A beads. Pass the needle under the thread bridge created in Step 1 and back up through the last two beads picked up. Pick up another two color A beads and anchor them to the same thread bridge so that three stacks of two beads sit side by side.

STEP 3

Working back in the opposite direction and using the same method, pick up four color A beads and anchor them to the second thread bridge created in Step 2. Pick up another two color A beads and anchor them to the first thread bridge created in the previous step. Then pick up two more color A beads and also anchor them to the first thread bridge created in the previous step.

STEP 4

For the next row, pick up two color B beads followed by two color A beads and anchor them to the third thread bridge created in Step 3. Then anchor two color A beads to the second thread bridge and two color A beads, followed by two B beads to the first thread bridge.

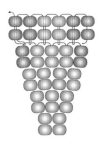

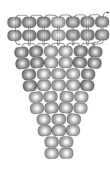

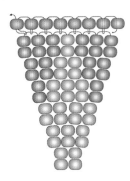

STEP 5

Work another row, starting with four color B beads anchored to the fourth thread bridge created in Step 4. Add two color A beads to the third bridge, two color A beads to the second thread bridge, and four color B beads to the first thread bridge (adding two beads at a time).

STEP 6

Work the final row of two-drop brick stitch, starting with four color B beads anchored to the fifth thread bridge created in Step 5. Add two color B beads to the fourth thread bridge, two color A beads to the third thread bridge, two color B beads to the second thread bridge, and four color B beads to the first thread bridge (adding two beads at a time).

STEP 7

Switch to single-drop brick stitch and work an increase row, adding eight color B beads.

New row

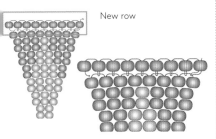

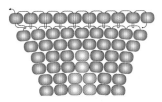

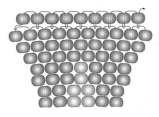

STEP 8

Work a second row of increasing single-drop brick stitch, adding nine color B beads.

STEP 9

Work a final row of increasing single-drop brick stitch, adding ten color B beads.

STEP 10

Begin a decrease row by picking up two color B beads and anchoring them to the eighth thread bridge created in Step 9 (skipping over the ninth thread bridge). Work the rest of the row, anchoring one color B bead to each of the remaining thread bridges, for a total of nine beads in this row.

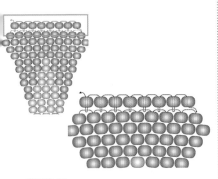

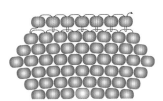

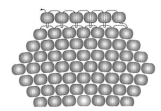

STEP 11

Using the same method as in Step 10, work another decrease row (skipping the final thread bridge created in Step 10), adding a total of eight color B beads.

STEP 12

Work another decrease row, adding a total of seven color B beads.

STEP 13

Work a final decrease row, adding a total of six color B beads.

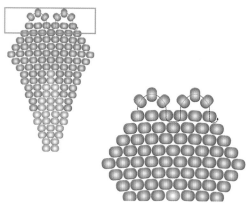

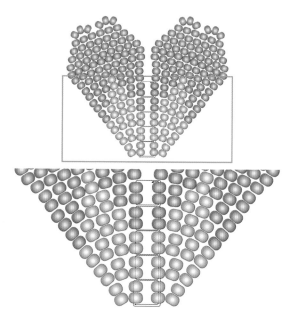

STEP 14

Pick up three color B beads and pass the needle down the fourth bead added in Step 13 and back up the third bead added in Step 13. Pick up three more color B beads and pass your needle down the first bead added in Step 13. Tie off and trim the working thread only. Repeat Steps 1–14 to make a total of nine petals, leaving the tail thread of each petal intact for later use.

STEP 15

Using one of the tail threads, attach two petals to each other by ladder stitching the outside edge beads of the first five rows together. Pull your thread firmly as you work, making sure that the petals are securely attached. Tie off and trim the tail thread you have just used, burying the knots in the body of the petal, leaving the other tail thread intact. Repeat to attach all nine petals together (including the remaining edges of petal 1 and petal 9) to form a flower. Tie off and trim any remaining threads.

STEP 17

Using the remaining thread, carefully attach the back of your flower to the top (domed section) of the sieve finding. Hold the flower in place on the sieve and pass the needle straight through the flower from front to back, out through a hole in the sieve, back through an adjacent hole, and through to the front of the flower. Pass the needle back through the flower and the sieve, making sure that the thread loops around an existing thread between the beads in the flower. Repeat this around the sieve and the flower (repeating a second time if necessary) so that the two parts are securely attached.

STEP 16

Tie in a new 60 in (152cm) length of thread, making sure to bury the knots in the centers of your petal. Travel through all the beads around the edge of your flower. Note that the picture shows two separate petals for clarity, but they will actually be attached by the bottom five rows. Pull your thread gently as you work so that the petals curve downward slightly.

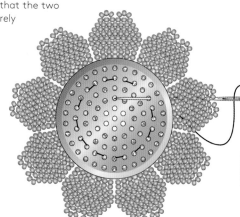

Kerrie Slade

1 QUICK WAY TO CREATE REALISTIC PETALS

- Two-drop brick stitch is worked exactly the same as regular (single-drop) brick stitch, except that you pick up two beads per stitch instead of one. Single-drop brick stitch results in slower-growing increases, whereas two-drop produces more dramatic increases. This allows you to create realistic-looking petals with a pointed base and a rounded tip.

3 WAYS TO WORK WITH THREAD AND KNOTS

- "Thread bridge" is a term used in brick stitch to describe the thread that connects two beads in a row. The beads in subsequent rows are held in place by passing the needle and thread under this bridge, which anchors the new beads in place.
- To avoid thread showing on the outside edge of your work, always pick up two beads (or two pairs/stacks if working in two-drop) together at the beginning of a row, but single beads/stacks for the rest of the stitches.
- Make sure that you place your knots in the body of the petal rather than around the outside edges, as you will need to be able to pass your needle freely through the edge beads later on.

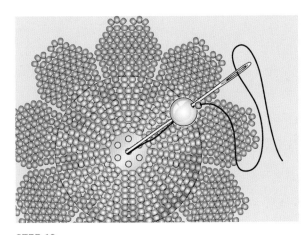

STEP 18
Using the same thread, pass the needle out through the central hole of the sieve finding and the center of the flower. Pick up the glass pearl and a color B bead. Pass the needle back through the pearl, the flower, and the central hole in the sieve. Turn and exit an adjacent hole in the sieve and retrace the thread path through the sieve, the pearl, and the new bead several times, making sure that the pearl is securely attached to the center of your flower. Tie off and trim the remaining thread.

STEP 19
Attach the pin part of the brooch finding to the sieve by carefully folding over the arms with the pliers.

FINISHED SIZE
2³/₄in (7cm) diameter

Glossary

2-DROP
When two or more beads are used at one time, but treated as though they are one bead.

AUGHT (OR "0")
A unit of measurement for seed beads. Originally based on how many beads fit into 1 in (2.5cm). Therefore, size 8 beads are bigger than size 15 beads.

AWG
American Wire Gauge. The measurement used to sell wire in the U.S.

BACK THROUGH
To thread back through a bead in the opposite direction.

BEAD REAMER
Tool used to enlarge or smooth bead holes.

BEZEL
A type of jewelry setting that is used to encircle and secure a stone or cabochon.

BRICK STITCH
Beading stitch in which the rows sit flat beside each other but are offset, to resemble brickwork.

BRIOLETTE WRAPPED LOOP (WRAPPED DROP)
A decorative and secure method of creating a loop on wire.

BUGLE BEAD
Long, tubular seed bead.

CHAIN-NOSE PLIERS
Pliers with flat inner jaws that taper to a point. Also called snipe-nose pliers.

CIRCLE THROUGH
To thread back through a bead in the same direction it originally went through.

CLAMSHELLS
Small findings, also called calottes, necklace tips, or necklace endings, used to hide unsightly knots in thread or to fasten the stringing material to the clasp.

CRIMP BEADS
Small metal beads that, when squashed with crimping pliers, bite into the nylon surface of flexible beading wire to secure.

CRIMPING
The act of squashing crimp beads to secure them onto flexible beading wire.

CRIMPING PLIERS
Pliers with two specially designed notches used to squash crimp beads.

CUBIC RIGHT-ANGLE WEAVE
Also known as CRAW, this is a cubic form of RAW used to make beadwork with four sides.

CULLING
Removing beads if they are misshapen, odd colors, or the wrong size.

DECREASING
Removing beads or stitches to narrow your work.

EYE PIN
A length of wire with a loop at one end.

FINDINGS
The small metal pieces used to finish jewelry, such as clasps, crimps, or earring hooks.

FLAT-NOSE PLIERS
Pliers with a flat inner jaw, the same width throughout.

FLEXIBLE BEADING WIRE
A series of very fine strands of stainless steel coated in nylon, used to string jewelry and to finish with crimp beads. Also called beading or stringing wire, or beading cable.

FREEFORM
A method of beading that uses any stitch or combination of stitches to create work that doesn't stick rigidly to the rules of any stitch.

FRENCH WIRE
Also called gimp or bullion, this is used to protect your thread from rubbing against metal findings.

GAUGE (GA)
A term used to indicate the thickness of wire.

HEADPIN
A length of wire with a wider end that stops beads from falling off.

HERRINGBONE STITCH
Decorative stitch in which the beads are added in pairs and resemble a herringbone pattern.

INCREASING
Adding extra beads or stitches to widen your work.

JUMP RING
Small loop of metal that can be used to attach findings.

LADDER STITCH
Basic beading stitch comprising of only one row of beads.

LAMPWORK
A technique for making handmade glass beads, using rods of glass heated in a flame and molded over a metal mandrel.

LOOM
The piece of equipment needed to bead loom work.

LOOM WORK
A method of beading that uses a loom to create flat pieces of beadwork in which the beads lie in neat rows.

MANDREL
A metal rod used to form jump rings or glass beads.

OFF-LOOM BEADWORK
Beadweaving stitches that are performed by hand without a loom. This includes peyote and brick stitch, as well as beaded chains and right-angle weave.

OVERHAND KNOT
A knot formed by making a loop in a piece of cord and pulling the end through it.

PEYOTE STITCH
Decorative stitch that creates a "fabric" of beads by weaving them together by hand in an offset row method.

RATTAIL
Satin cord made for beading projects.

RIGHT-ANGLE WEAVE
Also known as RAW, this is an off-loom stitch in which all the beads lie at right angles to each other.

ROUND-NOSE PLIERS
Pliers with rounded jaws that taper to a point.

SIMPLE LOOP
A small loop at the end of a wire. Also known as a rosary or turned loop.

SPLIT RING
These are used to attach findings to your jewelry.

SQUARE KNOT
Formed by tying a left-handed overhand knot and then a right-handed overhand knot, or vice versa. Also called a reef knot.

SQUARE STITCH
An off-loom beadweaving stitch that mimics the appearance of beadwork created on a loom. Each bead is connected by thread to each of the four beads surrounding it.

STEP UP
To finish a row of beadwork and ensure you're in the correct position to bead the next row.

STOP BEAD
Also called a tension bead. A bead added to the start of your work to stop other beads from falling off the thread, and to help you maintain tension.

TAIL THREAD
The end of thread that you leave at the start and end of your work to use to finish your beadwork.

TENSION
The tightness or looseness of your finished beadwork.

TUBULAR
Beadwork worked around a three-dimensional tubular shape.

ZIPPING UP
Joining the edges of a piece of flat beadwork to make it tubular (see page 145).

TABLE OF COMMON SEED BEADS

This table shows the vital statistics of a number of common bead sizes. This will give you an idea of the physical size of each of the bead sizes and the amount of beads per gram.

	Seed bead size	Beads per inch (2.5cm)	Approximate size	Number per 1 gram	Number per 10 grams	Number per 100 grams
	Size 15	24	1.5mm	250	2,500	25,000
	Size 11	18	2.2mm	120	1,200	12,000
	Size 8	13	3mm	36	360	3,600
	Size 6	10	3.7mm	18	180	1,800
	Cylinder bead size	Beads per inch (2.5cm)	Approximate size	Number per 1 gram	Number per 10 grams	Number per 100 grams
	Size 15	19	1.3mm	290	2,900	29,000
	Size 11	20	1.6mm	200	2,000	20,000

WIRE GAUGE

Wire is either sold in gauge (ga) or by millimeters (mm), both of which refer to its diameter. The gauge commonly used is American Wire Gauge (AWG). Although these don't match up exactly, a rough conversion is usually close enough for most wirework.

AWG	mm	AWG	mm
38	0.1	20	0.8
32	0.2	19	0.9
28	0.3	18	1
26	0.4	16	1.2
24	0.5	14	1.5
22	0.6	12	2
21	0.7		

HARD OR SOFT?

Wire is sold in different levels of hardness: soft; hard; and half-hard, each of which has its ideal uses.

Hardness	Ideal for	Unsuitable for
Soft	Wrapping around another wire—it won't harden and become brittle as you work it.	Making clasps or components—it will be too soft for the strength you need.
Hard	Making clasps and weight-bearing components—it has the strength to keep its shape.	Wrapping or any technique that requires a lot of work—the wire will become very difficult to manipulate and too hard on your hands.
Half-hard	All types of wirework—it is versatile. Don't choose half-hard if you need a really soft or hard wire, but otherwise it is an ideal substitute.	

COMMON BEAD SHAPES

Not all beads are round. They come in many shapes and sizes. Here are some of the most common, with their names and how their holes lie.

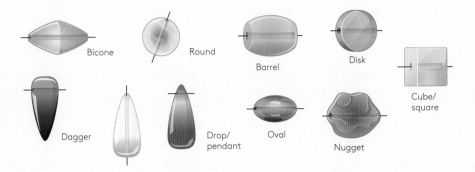

Bicone · Round · Barrel · Disk · Dagger · Drop/pendant · Oval · Nugget · Cube/square

ESTIMATING QUANTITIES

You'll find that the size of beads varies according to manufacturer, bead finish, and even color. This table shows an approximation of the average sizes and quantities.

	Bead (approximate size)	Beads per 1 in (2.5cm)	Beads per 18 in (46cm)	Beads per 24 in (61cm)
•	Size 15 seed bead (1.5mm)	17	307	401
••	Size 11 seed bead (1.8–2.2mm)	12–14	210–256	278–339
•	Size 8 seed bead (3.3mm)	8	140	185
•	Size 6 seed bead (4mm)	6	115	153
•	2mm bead	12	230	305
•	3mm bead	8	154	203
•	4mm bead	6	115	153
•	5mm bead	5	92	122
•	6mm bead	4	77	102
•	8mm bead	3	57	76
•	10mm bead	2	46	61
•	12mm bead	2	38	51
•	13mm bead	2	35	47

	Bead (approximate size)	Beads per 1 in (2.5cm)	Beads per 18 in (46cm)	Beads per 24 in (61cm)
	14mm bead	1–2	33	43
	15mm bead	1	30	40
	16mm bead	1	29	38
	17mm bead	1	27	36
	18mm bead	1	25	34
	20mm bead	1	23	30

Index

Credits

Thank you to all the beaders and other artists
who support and inspire me, and to my partner,
he who knows who he is.

Quarto would like to thank The Land of Odds bead store,
which generously provided the beads for pages 10–11:

Land of Odds—Be Dazzled Beads   www.landofodds.com

Quarto would like to thank the following for
supplying images for inclusion in this book:

r = right; l = left; c = center; t = top; b = bottom

Airs, Jennifer, www.jdjewellery.co.uk, pp.99bl,
100tl

Bevan, Shona, www.shonabevan.com, pp.99tl,
146–147, 148–149

Blackburn, Carol, www.carolblackburn.co.uk,
pp.24br

Carson, Lynda, Fresh Baked Designs, www.
freshbakeddesigns.wordpress.com, pp.22bl, 24tl,
56tl, 58tr

Davy, Lynn, www.lynndavybeadwork.co.uk,
pp.22br, 25bl/r, 52–53, 54–55, 99tr, 100br, 109t

Dell, Norma Jean, www.njdesigns1.com, pp.98br,
99br, 100bl, 101tl, 123t, 132b, 133t

Hook, Abby, www.abbyhook.co.uk, pp.59bl,
92–93, 94–95

Houston, Kimberly, www.thepinkmartini.etsy.com,
pp.22tr, 25tl, 31b

Jones, Linda, www.wirejewellery.co.uk, pp.56br,
57, 58br

Lock, Jane, pp.101tr, 101br

Millodot, Suzen, www.ornamental-knots.com,
pp.48–49, 50–51

New, Marie, p.98tr

Nolan, Sian, www.etsy.com/shop/SianNolan,
pp.98tl/bl, 100tr, 101bl

Perlic, Eleonora, www.etsy.com/shop/
SimplyWireWrapped, pp.56bl, 59tr

Pham, Huan, p.59tl

Poupazis, Chris & Joy, www.cjpoupazis.com,
pp.22tl, 23, 24tr/bl

Poyser, Debbie, https://weaversfield.etsy.com,
pp.56tr, 58bl, 59br

Slade, Kerrie, www.kerrieslade.co.uk, pp.150–151,
152–153

Smith, Kristin, www.ksjewellerydesigns.co.uk,
pp.58tl, 88–89, 90–91